BARRON'S
NEW JERSEY

ASK 8
LANGUAGE ARTS LITERACY TEST

THIRD EDITION

Oona Abrams, M.A.
Former English Teacher
Pascack Valley High School
Hillsdale, New Jersey

Tim Hassall, M.A.
President, HASS SAT Test Prep
Cherry Hill, New Jersey

IMPORTANT NOTE: Barron's has made every effort to ensure the content of this book is accurate as of press time, but New Jersey state exams are constantly changing. Be sure to consult **www.state.nj.us/education/assessment** for all the latest New Jersey state testing information. Regardless of the changes that may be announced after press time, this book will still provide a very strong framework for eighth-grade students preparing for the exam.

© Copyright 2013, 2009 by Barron's Educational Series, Inc.
Previous edition © Copyright 2006 by Barron's Educational Series, Inc.
under the title *New Jersey GEPA Language Arts Literacy*.

All inquiries should be addressed to:
Barron's Educational Series, Inc.
250 Wireless Boulevard
Hauppauge, New York 11788
www.barronseduc.com

ISBN: 978-1-4380-0246-0

ISSN 2324–7592

10%
POST-CONSUMER
WASTE
Paper contains a minimum
of 10% post-consumer
waste (PCW). Paper used
in this book was derived
from certified, sustainable
forestlands.

PRINTED IN THE UNITED STATES OF AMERICA
9 8 7 6 5 4 3 2 1

Contents

UNDERSTANDING THE ASK 8

INTRODUCTION

This book is intended for use both in and out of the middle school classroom. It is an excellent resource for test review and skills assessments. The exercises in this book offer students the opportunity to strengthen the essential literacy and writing skills an eighth grader needs to enter high school. Teachers can easily incorporate the material in this book into their lesson plans, not only at test preparation time but also throughout the school year.

WHAT IS THE ASK 8?

The "ASK" in ASK 8 stands for Assessment of Skills and Knowledge. The state of New Jersey has to make sure every eighth grader has the skills necessary for success in high school. So the ASK 8 evaluates whether or not you have the necessary skills to enter high school.

WHAT YOUR SCORE MEANS

Scoring ranges from 100 to 300. If you score above 250, you are considered Advanced Proficient. If you score above 200, you are Proficient. If you score below 200, you're Partially Proficient. Because the laws governing the state require you to be Proficient, you may be required to take a remedial class in ninth grade to better your skills. Scoring above 200 should be every eighth grader's goal!

Does My Score Really Show If I Am Ready for High School?

The ASK 8 evaluates three major skills:

1. Your critical reading skills
2. Your ability to write clearly and maturely
3. Your potential to be an independent thinker

All three skills are essential not only in high school, not only in college, but also in LIFE!

HOW THE TEST IS SET UP

The test has four major sections:

1. Speculative Writing *or* Explanatory Writing
2. Informational Text
3. Narrative Text
4. Persuasive Essay

At the time of this book's publication, these four sections were the primary ones used for evaluation. Sometimes sections are changed, updated, or removed. For example, an essay correction section was once on the test and now no longer is. The NJ ASK will be replaced in the coming years as New Jersey adopts new national standards for learning. Your teachers will help you prepare for all sections of the ASK 8.

WHAT IS THE SPECULATIVE WRITING SECTION?

The speculative prompt requires you to examine a question or situation closely and tell a story based on it. It is the most creative section on the test, but it is not a free-for-all. This section assesses your ability to analyze, imagine, and articulate in writing the story behind a text.

WHAT IS THE EXPLANATORY WRITING SECTION?

The explanatory writing prompt gives a statement and asks you to respond to it. Unlike the persuasive essay, you do not have to take a pro or con position. Rather, you need to interpret the prompt and explain it with good supporting examples.

WHAT IS THE INFORMATIONAL TEXT SECTION?

In this section, you will read a nonfiction article or essay. The author of the article or essay has a clear purpose—to convince you of his or her point of view. After you have read the article, you will answer eight multiple-choice questions and one open-ended question.

WHAT IS THE NARRATIVE TEXT SECTION?

Like the informational text section, this section also has both multiple-choice and open-ended questions. Unlike the informational text section, the text in this section will be fiction. It will be either a short story or a section of a longer piece of fiction.

On each narrative text section, you will answer ten multiple-choice questions and two open-ended questions. You will be given more time to complete the narrative text sections than you will for the informational text sections.

HOW DIFFICULT ARE THE MULTIPLE-CHOICE QUESTIONS?

Get ready. They are going to be somewhat challenging for a couple of reasons. The multiple-choice questions on the ASK 8 are different because they assess your on-the-spot reading abilities. You are reading under timed conditions. However, the one good thing about all the reading passage questions is that they are open book. You can (and should) look back at the text to find the answers!

WHAT IS THE PERSUASIVE WRITING SECTION?

In this section, you will be given a scenario that has two possible outcomes. You will write a five-paragraph persuasive essay or persuasive letter (depending on the scenario you are given). In this essay or letter, you will argue for one of the outcomes, giving three clear reasons in your three body paragraphs. This is the longest writing piece that you will have on the exam, so you really have to focus on doing the best job you possibly can. Chapter 6 offers detailed directions on everything you need to know to get a good score on the persuasive essay.

HOW STUDENT WRITING GETS GRADED

The appendix of this book includes the two rubrics that will be used to grade your writing on the ASK 8. You will be asked to refer to them throughout the course of your work in this book. Following the rubrics is a scoring chart that you can use to "grade" how well you performed on the two practice tests.

To break down the scoring, the six-point scale can be thought of like this:

6 = A+   5 = A   4 = B   3 = C   2 = D   1 = F

The four-point scale can be thought of like this:

4 = A   3 = B   2 = C   1 = D/F

This is a simple way of understanding how the writing is scored.

BENEFITS BEYOND THE TEST ITSELF

Do not consider this book just practice for the real test. Think about it as practice for high school. If you apply the skills you learn in this book, then you should be able to get the knack for tackling multiple-choice questions, essay tasks, and writing prompts. If you take the exercises in this book seriously, you should learn essential reading and writing skills for high school.

Chapter 2

APPROACHING THE SPECULATIVE PROMPT

YOUR CHANCE TO BE CREATIVE

The speculative prompt requires you to think creatively. For some students, this section of the test will be a breeze. For others, it will seem like torture. Using the situation and specific details given in the prompt, you will be asked to compose a story that incorporates them.

TIPS FOR EVALUATING A PROMPT

On this exam, you will be asked to complete a writing task on a very specific prompt in 30 minutes. This task will be either *speculative* or *explanatory* (the explanatory prompt will be covered in Chapter 3). The speculative prompt will be written in such a way that you are given a *scenario* to envision and imagine. The scenario will include the basic background of a story, and it will include a certain sequence of events that shows you a conflict that needs to be resolved. It is your chance to be creative and be a storyteller.

To do that, think about what you are given in the prompt, and think of the elements of what makes a good story:

- establishing the problem, or what will drive the story
- showing rising action as the story builds
- bringing the story to a climax
- concluding the story

Without these elements, you will not have a good story, and you will not score well on the prompt.

SPECULATING ABOUT TEXT

To *speculate* means to form a hypothesis or an educated guess. You will speculate what story lies behind the prompt. In social studies class, you use the Five Ws when you discuss a current event. When you speculate about a text, you must cover those same Five Ws:

- Who?
- What?
- When?
- Where?
- Why?

Each of the four sample prompts in this chapter is accompanied by a suggested planning strategy for prewriting. Although you are not officially graded on prewriting, the test makers provide you with planning space throughout the test. This space is provided because a good writer will take the time to plan and organize. You cannot score your best without planning first! Choose the prewriting strategy with which you are most comfortable. Keep in mind the scoring rubric, located in the appendix of this book. The easiest way to think of scoring rubric is as follows:

- 6 = A+
- 5 = A
- 4 = B
- 3 = C
- 2 = D
- 1 = F

When you think of the scoring this way, it is much easier to understand why essays receive certain scores. You have written many things over your years in school, and now you are being asked to show off your skills.

Have a Strategy

Because you are given only 30 minutes to write this piece, you must have a plan of action going into the test. You must practice beforehand to see which strategy is best for you. Pay close attention to the sample essays following each of the practice essay prompts. The ASK 8 rubric is designed to reward you for what you do well and give you every opportunity to succeed at the task. Remember, you can write either a creative story or an expository essay as long as your central focus answers the questions who? what? when? where? why? and how? about the prompt you are given.

The test rewards students who take **compositional risk.** When you try something different and do not write the same type of essay or story many other students write, you are taking compositional risk. If you have heard the term "think outside the box," you understand what compositional risk is. Try to approach your essay in an unconventional way, or tell your story with a twist that the reader will not see coming. Doing this makes the writing more enjoyable and, therefore, better.

SHOW, DON'T TELL

Another way to make your writing better is to show what is happening, not tell it. Consider the following examples.

Example One:

Little Red Riding Hood did not recognize her grandmother. She asked her about her physical features until the wolf, disguised as her grandmother, announced that he was going to eat her.

Example Two:

Little Red Riding Hood approached her grandmother. "Grandma, what big eyes you have!" she exclaimed.

"The better to see you with," the Wolf, disguised as her grandmother, replied.

"And what a big nose you have!" Red Riding Hood said.

"The better to smell you with," said the Wolf.

"And what big teeth you have!" Red Riding Hood exclaimed.

"The better to eat you with!" cried the Wolf as he leaped out of the bed.

SPECULATIVE COMPOSITION PROMPT #1

Directions: You are going out to a nice restaurant. Where would you go? What would you order? Using your imagination and experience, picture a scenario that takes these ideas as its basis. Then write your story. You have 30 minutes.

METHOD #1: USING A CHART

Examine the planning chart that follows. Charting is a good technique to use if you like to write lists. Then you can organize your thoughts based on the ideas you've jotted down. Notice that the questions who? what? when? where? why? and how? are all addressed in this chart. Now look at the sample essay that has been written from this prewriting.

- **Who?** The narrator (Jasmine) and her date (Anthony)
- **What?** Dinner date
- **Where?** La Terraza, the fanciest restaurant in town
- **When?** A romantic evening
- **Why?** Unless a couple at another table ruins it

"Thank you, sir," my date, the handsome Anthony, told the waiter as he took our orders to the kitchen.

La Terraza was the best restaurant in town, and Anthony had asked me on a date there. Anthony was kind, smart, and polite. My parents had not been there to meet him because they decided to go out themselves since I wouldn't be home.

"Well," I thought, "they'll get to meet him when we get home at least."

"Jasmine, I wanted to tell you something. Well, ask you something," Anthony started.

I felt goose pimples on my arms and hoped Anthony didn't notice.

"Jasmine, will . . ."

His voice trailed away as another noise filled our ears. A loud laugh broke the calm of the dining room. The high booth next to us made it hard to see whoever had made that annoying laugh. And the next. And the one after that.

"What was that?" I asked.

"Sounds like someone's having a good time," Anthony said. "Like me." He smiled.

I smiled back, trying to forget our obnoxious neighbors. But their sounds grew louder, and their booth shifted, bumping into us. They were apparently having a good time, but too good of a time. I couldn't take it anymore. No one was going to ruin this moment. "I'll be right back," I said.

"Jasmine, please," Anthony pleaded. "Don't ruin our date."

"It will only take a second," I said.

I took a breath, stood up, and turned the corner of the booth. "You annoying, obnoxious . . ."

I stopped. No more words came from my mouth. I swallowed and tried again. "Hi, Mom and Dad."

They were not amused. As I turned around, Anthony was gone. I was wrong. He wouldn't get to meet my parents after all.

COMMENTARY

This imaginary narrative would earn a score of 5. Note how the writer used dialogue to tell the story. Also note the compositional risk: the obnoxious couple turns out to be the narrator's parents. This twist takes the story beyond the ordinary and boosts the score.

SPECULATIVE COMPOSITION PROMPT #2

Directions: You are quite surprised when one day you meet a famous person. Who do you meet? When? Under what circumstances? What is the story behind this scenario? Drawing on your imagination and experience, construct a scene using this idea or narrate what is happening. Then write your story. You have 30 minutes.

METHOD #2: USING A GRAPHIC ORGANIZER

Graphic organizers and flowcharts help writers to unpack meaning and answer questions before they begin writing. During each step, the writer is able to think on paper. Using prompt #2, fill in the graphic organizer that follows.

Story Flowchart

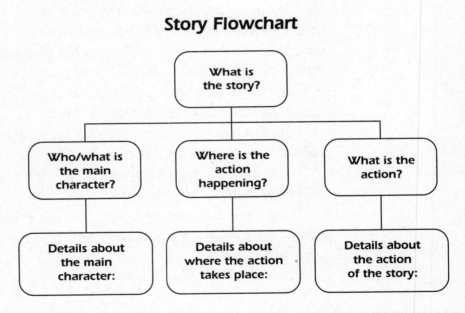

Each idea in your graphic organizer should lead to an extension or further development. In this exercise, you are literally stretching your mind for the possibilities of the story. Look at the sample essay that follows and the prewriting graphic organizer that precedes it. Can you see the connections between the graphic organizer and the essay?

Story Flowchart

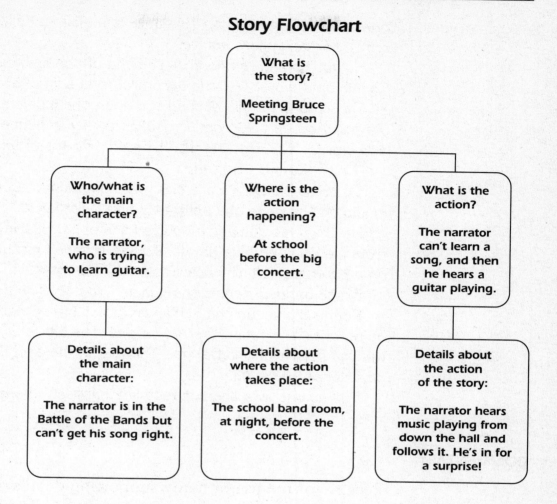

What is
the story?

Meeting Bruce
Springsteen

Who/what is
the main
character?

The narrator,
who is trying
to learn guitar.

Where is the
action
happening?

At school
before the big
concert.

What is the
action?

The narrator
can't learn a
song, and then
he hears a
guitar playing.

Details about
the main
character:

The narrator is in the
Battle of the Bands but
can't get his song right.

Details about
where the action
takes place:

The school band room,
at night, before the
concert.

Details about
the action
of the story:

The narrator hears
music playing from
down the hall and
follows it. He's in for
a surprise!

"Ugh! I can't get this chord right!" Ronnie screamed in frustration. He had been practicing for an hour now but was still stuck on the first page, trying to read the music and make his fingers play the chords. Tonight was the Battle of the Bands, but if Ronnie couldn't get these chords right, not only would his band, the Little Giants, lose, but they would also be the laughingstock of Springfield High School.

As he picked up his guitar again, he thought he heard something. Ronnie put down the guitar and went to the door of the band room. A familiar sound was coming from down the hall. Not just familiar—it was the song his band was set to play, "Born to Run", only it was being played perfectly.

Following the music, Ronnie decided that whoever was playing could show him a thing or two. As he walked downstairs, he thought, "This sure is a gloomy hallway. I never remember being here before."

He got to a green door at the end of the hallway. "Weird," Ronnie said aloud. "All the other doors in school are white."

The second Ronnie opened the door, the music stopped playing. Across the room, Bruce Springsteen himself turned and smiled. "My first big hit," he said. "Born to Run."

"How?" Ronnie started.

Bruce motioned Ronnie over. "It's not about seeing the music on the page," he said. "It's about feeling it."

He lifted his guitar and played the song. Hearing it come from his voice and his hands, Ronnie stopped picturing chords on a page and felt the power and emotion of it.

Bruce handed Ronnie the guitar. "You try," he said.

Ronnie picked up the guitar and shut his eyes. By the time he reached the second verse, he knew the Little Giants would win the Battle of the Bands. "Thank you," he said softly when he finished the song.

But no one was there. Bruce Springsteen was gone.

COMMENTARY

Because of the use of many supporting details, this speculative essay would earn a score of 6. The writer takes compositional risk with the meeting of a famous rock star under mysterious circumstances, and then the mystery is heightened when the rock star disappears. Was it real after all?

SPECULATIVE COMPOSITION PROMPT #3

Directions: Imagine going back in time. What time would you go to? Whom do you meet? What would you see? Under what circumstances? What is the story behind this scenario? Use your imagination and experience to explain what the story is about or to narrate what is happening. Then write your story. You have 30 minutes.

METHOD #3: USING AN OUTLINE

If you tend to be a logical or mathematical learner, the outline will suit you. It is an organized and simple method for you to gather your thoughts. Be careful, though! Some people do not outline properly, or they don't understand the importance of sequencing. Do not confuse outlining with listing. The best form of outlining to use when writing a story is the one that is often used to dissect a story that is being read. It follows this format:

STORY OUTLINE

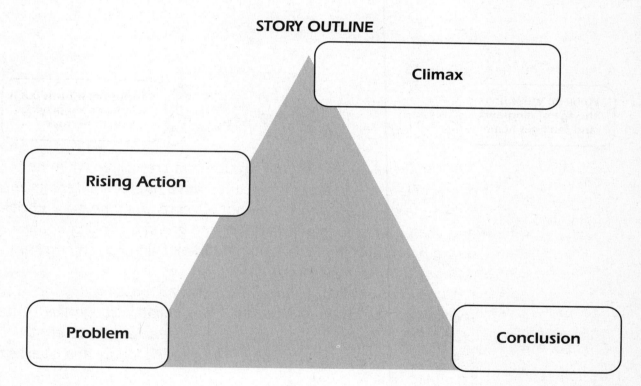

Now practice writing a sample outline for the prompt on page 12.

STORY OUTLINE

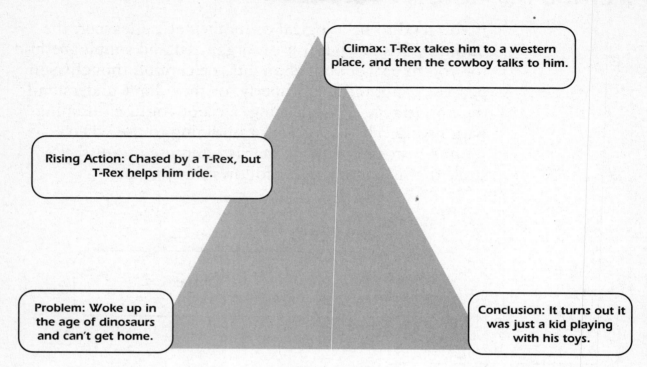

Climax: T-Rex takes him to a western place, and then the cowboy talks to him.

Rising Action: Chased by a T-Rex, but T-Rex helps him ride.

Problem: Woke up in the age of dinosaurs and can't get home.

Conclusion: It turns out it was just a kid playing with his toys.

Billy awoke to the ground around him trembling. When he opened his eyes, he saw ferns and plants he did not recognize. He was in a forest, and it was hot. Overhead, he heard a shriek and then saw a huge shadow over the ground. Looking up, he saw a pterodactyl. A dinosaur? The last thing he remembered was being in his bedroom.

"I have to get out of here," he mumbled, getting up. The trembling got closer, and then a T-Rex burst through the trees. The monster looked around. As it was about to spot Billy, Billy started to run. The T-Rex growled loudly and started to chase him.

As Billy ran, he looked back, seeing if he had put any distance between them. He saw the dinosaur's eye. It looked sad, almost as if it was looking more for a friend than a meal. "It's a dinosaur. He wants to eat me," he told himself.

Just then, he tripped over a big tree root. He hit the ground hard and blacked out.

When Billy awoke, he was no longer in the forest. He was in a saloon, and in through its swinging doors walked a cowboy.

So many questions filled Billy's head. What happened? How did I get here? Where's the T-Rex?

As he walked through the swinging doors to head outside, he bumped into another cowboy.

"Hey there, partner," the cowboy said. "You new to these here parts?"

Before Billy could reply, the cowboy continued. "I'm the sheriff around here, and I've got to find the owner of this here big horse. It's blocking the whole street and scaring the townsfolk."

Billy followed the cowboy's finger, which was pointing to a T-Rex, a saddle on its giant back, in the middle of the dusty road.

"Billy! Supper's ready!" the cowboy said. Only it wasn't the cowboy.

"OK, Mom!" Billy said. "Be right down!"

He turned to his cowboy doll and T-Rex plastic animal. "Don't leave just yet, partner," he said.

COMMENTARY

The action of this speculative essay unfolds without ever giving away the ending. The idea of it all being in a child's mind is clever, but it's not too much of a stretch to say that it has been done before. It scores a 5.

SPECULATIVE COMPOSITION PROMPT #4

Directions: One day a teenager deceives someone. What might happen? Drawing on your imagination, construct a scene using this idea or narrate what is happening.
Then write your story. You have 30 minutes.

METHOD #4: ORGANIZING FROM BRAINSTORMING NOTES

If you are the type of learner who needs a bit more freedom to organize and feels limited by charts and graphs, starting with a general brainstorm and working from those notes might best suit you. You know that your composition needs to have a clear introduction, organization, and closure, but you also know that you need freedom to come up with good ideas. Many students just jot down a bulleted list of notes in response to the prompt. Others need to create a web of ideas and visually branch out their thoughts on a blank sheet of paper. Whatever your situation might be, the most important thing to remember is to "think on paper" BEFORE you write your official composition. Too many students put their brainstorming notes into their compositions instead of using them to help organize their composition.

SAMPLE BRAINSTORMING LIST:

Reasons a teen might deceive his or her parents:

- going to a party
- skipping school
- hanging out with the wrong people
- driving carelessly

Now decide what you want to discuss in your essay. Remember, you have only 30 minutes to write, and you have a little more prewriting to do. Choose what you will be able to write about specifically in the allotted time. In this case, the writer chose the following two topics:

- going to a party
- driving safely

The writer then created a new list of details to discuss under each general topic:

Going to a party:
- Not safe
- Parents don't know

Driving safely:
■ Cars are dangerous
■ Teens aren't allowed to have more than one other in a car

Whether your choice is a list or a map, you will be well prepared to start writing your composition now.

"Hey, Nicole! Get my note?" asked Jordan. "I told her to give it to you in science."

"Hey Jordan," Nicole said. "Didn't see her in science. I was making up that test in the lab room."

"Jake is having this huge party tonight. He invited me and told me to bring you. Chris will be there."

"I have to go!" Jordan said. "Oh, no no no. My parents will never let me."

Nicole stared at her. "Are you kidding? Tell them you're staying at my house tonight."

"You know I can't lie, Nicole."

"You can be honest and stay home, or lie and see Chris," Nicole said.

"I don't know," Jordan said. She pictured Chris. "All right, I'll tell them I'm staying at your house. They'll never know."

"Great! Chris will pick us up at my house at eight."

"I'll be there," Jordan said.

Jordan couldn't think of anything besides Chris and the party for the rest of the day. But she had one thing left to do.

"Hey, Mom. It's OK if I stay at Nicole's tonight, right?"

Jordan's mom said, "Sure. You girls have fun!"

It made Jordan sick lying to her mom like that, but she tried to put it out of her mind by picking out her outfit and putting on her makeup. She was out the door at 7:30.

At 8:00, a car beeped out front. Nicole and Jordan raced out front to Chris's blue Scion.

They were stopped at a light. When the light turned green, Chris said, "Watch this!" and hit the gas.

But Chris lost control of the wheel, and the car started to skid across the road. There would be no party. No good time. No hanging out with Chris. If only . . .

"You can be honest and stay home, or lie and see Chris," Nicole said.

Jordan thought of it all, and then thought of her parents. "I think," she said, "I'll be honest."

COMMENTARY

This speculative essay shows the consequences of lying, but the compositional risk of it all happening in the main character's mind in a moment gives it a hopeful, happy ending. It scores a 5.

CHAPTER REVIEW

- Plan and prewrite before you write your essay using any of the formats shown in this chapter. Even though you are not graded on your prewriting, three to five minutes of planning will pay off when you write your essay.
- Whatever method of prewriting you choose, make sure that you use a clear method of organization that works best for you.
- Show, don't tell, what is happening. Let the reader figure things out.
- Try compositional risk. Try something different. Think outside the box to make a story that is beyond the ordinary.

Chapter 3

APPROACHING THE EXPLANATORY PROMPT

RESPONDING TO A STATEMENT

For many years, the eighth grade test included two main writing components: a persuasive essay and a speculative prompt. Recently, the Department of Education decided that students should be prepared for a third kind of prompt, an explanatory essay prompt. This prompt is similar to the persuasive prompt in that students must take a stand and back it up, and it is similar to the speculative prompt in that students have only 30 minutes to complete the task.

*The NJ ASK 8 always has a persuasive essay. It also has **either** a **speculative prompt** or an **explanatory prompt.** It does not contain both prompts. However, since there is no way of knowing what kind of prompt the test will contain, it is essential to prepare for all three kinds of writing prompts.*

TIPS FOR EVALUATING A PROMPT

On this exam, you will be asked to complete a writing task on a very specific prompt in 30 minutes. If your prompt is an explanatory prompt, you will be given a statement, usually a quote, to read. Then you will have 30 minutes to compose a structured essay explaining what the quotation means to you.

To begin, think about these elements in the prompt and think how the quote might apply to your own life:

- Are there people and events you have learned about in school that exemplify the statement?
- Have there been times in your own life when the prompt has applied to you?
- Do you know anyone (a friend or family member) who has a story that would exemplify the prompt?

Thinking of past experiences will give you the brainstorming you will need to respond to the prompt.

EXPLAINING ABOUT TEXT

As in the previous chapter on speculative prompts, each of the three sample prompts in this chapter is accompanied by a suggested planning strategy for prewriting. Again, you are provided with planning space, but what you prewrite is up to you. Remember, the worst kind of prewriting is no prewriting at all! Keep in mind the scoring rubric, located in the appendix of this book. Again, the easiest way to think of the scoring rubric is as follows:

- 6 = A+
- 5 = A
- 4 = B
- 3 = C
- 2 = D
- 1 = F

Understanding how essays are scored can help you set your own goal scorewise.

HAVE A STRATEGY

Because you are given only 30 minutes to write this piece, you must have a plan of action going into the test. You must practice beforehand to see which strategy is best for you. Read the sample essays following each of the practice essay prompts to see what kind of writing receives a top score.

Remember, too, that the test rewards students who take a **compositional risk**. When you try something different and do not write the same type of essay or story many other students write, you are taking compositional risk. Again, try to approach your essay in a way that the reader will not expect. When you do this, it makes the writing more enjoyable and, therefore, better.

EXPLANATORY COMPOSITION PROMPT #1

Directions: Ben Franklin once said, "Today is yesterday's pupil." Think about what this quote means to you. Then plan and write an essay explaining your thoughts. You have 30 minutes.

METHOD #1: USING A GRAPHIC ORGANIZER

Graphic organizers and flow charts help writers to unpack meaning and answer questions before they begin writing. During each step, the writer is able to think on paper while the organizer arranges the thoughts. Using prompt #1, fill in the graphic organizer that follows.

Important: Because you are given only 30 minutes to complete the prompt, it is not necessary to write five paragraphs to receive a good score. A fifth paragraph with strong details can help you achieve a top (6) score, but you can receive a 5 with only four paragraphs. It is better to have four strong paragraphs than five weak ones. Since the third supporting paragraph is not essential, it will be included in the prewriting but not necessarily in the essay.

Explanatory Organizer

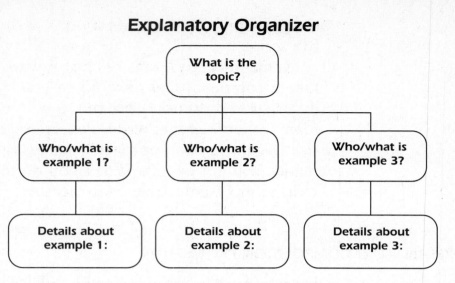

Each idea in your graphic organizer should lead to details that back up the example. These are specifics that will make your writing more precise. Look at the sample graphic organizer and then read the essay that follows it. Can you see the connections between the graphic organizer and the essay?

Completed Explanatory Organizer

What is the topic?

You can learn from the past.

Who/what is example 1?	Who/what is example 2?	Who/what is example 3?
Personal experience.	Inventors.	

Details about example 1:	Details about example 2:	Details about example 3:
School assignments—Lewis and Clark project.	Edison—lightbulb.	Fashion, medicines.

The past is important. When you get to your future, it will have been determined by all those decisions you made in your past. Ben Franklin's quote, "Today is yesterday's pupil," explains that you learn from your past mistakes.

I have learned that everyone has made mistakes in their lives, things they regret and things they learn lessons from. Last year I had a big social studies project due. We had two weeks to complete it, but I always put it off, thinking I could stay up and complete it all in one night. When that night came, though, I realized that I had not done the research I needed on Lewis and Clark. When I started to look them up on the computer, I was overwhelmed with the amount of information I found. There was no way I could get the project done on time. Having to face my teacher and tell her that my project was not done was bad, but what was worse was knowing it was my fault. I vowed never to put off an assignment again, and to this day, I haven't.

Inventors are people who learn from the past. Usually, inventors fail many times before they get the product they want. Each time an invention fails, the inventor learns why it fails and works to improve it. Their past experiments tell them what to change. Thomas Edison tried over a thousand experiments to get the lightbulb just right, with a filament that would last. When Edison learned from his mistakes, we all benefited. The light in the room right now is a result of Edison being yesterday's pupil.

In order to make a better today, and therefore a better future, you must make mistakes. "To err is human," as they say. There is a reason for that. Only from making mistakes can we learn and change. Mistakes are full of lessons just waiting to be learned.

COMMENTARY

Because of the use of specific supporting details, this explanatory essay would earn a score of 5. There is some compositional risk when the writer mentions the light in the room, reminding the reader what the writer is doing and why, while still making a valid point about the essay topic.

EXPLANATORY COMPOSITION PROMPT #2

Directions: René Descartes said, "It is not enough to have a good mind. The main thing is to use it well." Think about what this quote means to you. Then plan and write an essay explaining your thoughts. You have 30 minutes.

METHOD #2: USING AN OUTLINE

An outline not only puts your thoughts on paper, it also gives those ideas structure. An explanatory essay outline, remember, can have four or five paragraphs depending on how much time it takes you to outline and write.

Essay Outline
I Introduction
  A) Detail
  B) Thesis
II First Supporting Paragraph
  A) Detail
III Second Supporting Paragraph
  A) Detail
IV Third Supporting Paragraph
  A) Detail
V Conclusion
  A) Restate topic
  B) Wrap up

Now practice writing a sample outline for the prompt above.

Essay Outline
I Introduction
  A) Detail: Descartes quote.
  B) Thesis: Just because you're smart doesn't give you the excuse to not try.
II First Supporting Paragraph
  A) Friend Abby smart but doesn't try hard.
  B) Could do better but doesn't try.

III Second Supporting Paragraph
   A) Father—grew up poor but got into college.
   B) Now he's a doctor.
IV Third Supporting Paragraph
   A) Ben Franklin
   B) Smart but worked hard—post office, university, fire department.
V Conclusion
   A) It's not enough to be smart.
   B) If you're smart, you should try harder.

René Descartes once said, "It is not enough to have a good mind. The main thing is to use it well." This is a smart quote from a smart man. For us to understand it, we must ourselves follow what he said. Just because you are smart does not excuse you from trying hard.

In school, I have a close friend named Abby. She's in my grade and in many of my classes. When we play games where mind power is needed, she always outsmarts me. If you give her a puzzle, she is fast to conquer it. However, she does not understand Descartes' quote. She does not always use her mind well in school. Abby could easily be a straight A student if she wanted to, but she does not always pay attention in class. She also never does her homework or studies for tests and so gets Cs when she could be making the honor roll. Giving Abby a good brain is a waste since she never uses it well.

My father is another example of Descartes' quote, but in the opposite way. He was born poor in a poor city. Although he is smart, he had to work extremely hard at school to get great grades because he knew he would need scholarships to help him get through college. That hard work did pay off, and he went on to medical school. Even though he became a doctor, he still works hard every day. He told me that he wants to be the best doctor for his patients, and not keeping up with new techniques would mean he is not being the best. My father has a brilliant mind, and he puts it to good use.

Benjamin Franklin is also a great example of Descartes' quote. Franklin worked hard his whole life, making a good living in publishing, although he was not rich. But he always pushed his mind in other directions. He founded a university (Penn), the post office, and a fire department. He experimented with electricity. He invented a stove that heated better and bifocal glasses. This was the work of a man who never let his mind rest. Franklin, being a publisher, must have read Descartes, and if he did, he definitely took what he said to heart.

Being smart does not give you the excuse to sit back and let things come easily to you. There is no excuse for being lazy and not trying your best. In fact, being given the gift of a smart brain should be all the more reason to try harder. If the routine is easy for you, push your brain to its limits. Otherwise, as Descartes knew, you are wasting that gift.

COMMENTARY

This explanatory essay contains three examples with excellent details about the quote. The writer also took compositional risk, first by assuming Franklin must have read Descartes, and second in writing in the conclusion that a smart brain should be pushed harder. This essay scores a 6.

EXPLANATORY COMPOSITION PROMPT #3

Directions: "If you find a path with no obstacles, it probably doesn't lead anywhere." Think about what this quote means to you. Then plan and write an essay explaining your thoughts. You have 30 minutes.

METHOD #3: BRAINSTORMING

If you are more of a freethinker, you might think that outlining restricts you. If that is the case, it is still important to get your ideas down on paper before you begin writing. A bulleted list or a web of ideas can be enough for some people to write a good paper. However you do your prewriting, remember that any prewriting is better than none.

SAMPLE BRAINSTORMING LIST:

A path with no obstacles does not lead anywhere:

- easy way not the best way
  - travel soccer—got cut then worked harder
- get used to not being fair
- hard way builds character
  - Mother Theresa
- no challenge in easy way
- easy way is a trick to thinking life is easy
  - brother in college—friend is at home and bored

Whether you do this as a list or as a map, you are well prepared to start writing your composition now:

Two college students. One goes out and parties all the time and doesn't study. The other studies, works hard, and gets As and Bs. While the first student might be having more fun, those fun times only last for a short while. Which path is better? The quote "If you find a path with no obstacles, it probably doesn't lead anywhere" tells me to always take the smartest way and never take the easy road.

First, the easy way doesn't challenge you. If there's no challenge, there's no gain, either. Obstacles, although hard, teach us lessons. When I did not make the travel team in soccer, I took it as a challenge to try harder and train harder. This year, when I made the team, the reward was so much greater. The path with no obstacles does not prepare you for any failure, which will only end with a big crash.

Also, the harder way is the better way. The only way to become a better person is through hardship. It gets you used to the world not being fair and full of hard times. Mother Theresa is generally regarded as a saint because she chose the hard path. She went to the slums in India and worked with the poorest of the poor. That hard work paid off because she helped thousands of others to have better lives, and she herself became a role model to the world. She did not choose the path with no obstacles.

Last, you cannot go anywhere in life if your path doesn't lead anywhere. The easy way is a trick that people get fooled by. No obstacles means no challenges, and no challenges means no rewards, either. For example, my brother Jim worked hard and is now at college studying to be an engineer. His friend Dave did not work hard, and now he is home while all of his other friends are away. Dave has stopped by our house and talked to me and my parents even though Jim isn't home because he is bored. Dave's easy path led him nowhere. Hopefully now he'll choose a harder path.

In conclusion, the quote is advice for us all. If we are not challenged, then we will find no reward either. We will not become better people. The harder way is actually the better way. So when it's your turn to choose, what will you do, the easy way or the hard way?

COMMENTARY

This explanatory essay shows the consequences of taking the easy way and the reward of taking the hard way. The author writes three strong supporting paragraphs with good detail. It scores a 6.

CHAPTER REVIEW

- The explanatory essay is the newest writing prompt on the NJ ASK 8. It gives you a statement and asks you to respond with an essay in 30 minutes.
- The explanatory prompt may be on the test, or there may be a speculative prompt, but not both. However, you have to be prepared for both since you do not know which kind of prompt you will see.
- As with every other kind of extended writing, prewriting is essential. Use a method of organizing your thoughts that works for you.
- Remember, the explanatory essay can be four or five paragraphs. It is better to have four strong, detailed paragraphs then five brief ones. Practice writing the essays and see how much you can plan and write in 30 minutes.

Chapter 4

INFORMATIONAL AND NARRATIVE TEXT PRACTICE EXERCISES

UNDERSTANDING THE SETUP

Each of the passages in this chapter is followed by a set of multiple-choice questions and open-ended questions. Although the key for the multiple-choice questions is at the end of this chapter, the open-ended questions will be addressed in detail in Chapter 5. Write your answers to the open-ended questions on a separate sheet of paper. Remember that each open-ended question will require you to write two paragraphs. That means you will write a total of four paragraphs to answer the two open-ended questions at the end of each passage. Be sure to label each open-ended question with its corresponding number. In addition, be sure to write your own answers before looking at the sample responses in Chapter 5.

If your school has a writing center, visit it and ask a teacher or a peer tutor to help you. The best way to practice for the open-ended questions on the ASK 8 is to do as many timed reading and writing exercises as possible.

TIPS FOR APPROACHING MULTIPLE-CHOICE QUESTIONS

1. Remember that the author of a text wants to argue a point. Always keep that point in mind as you read the text and answer the questions. Sometimes, the point will be controversial. At other times, it will be a basic idea.

2. The author of a narrative text wants to offer a message to his or her readers. That message, or theme, is the main idea of the narrative text. Usually, the theme is a life lesson.

3. Before you read the text, look over the multiple-choice questions. Mark any specific text references in the questions immediately. Pay close attention to these areas as you read.

4. As you read each text, *you must take notes* in the margins and on the text itself. This is difficult for some students to get used to because they usually don't write in their books or on their handouts from teachers. Get into the habit now. Even if you think you will do well without taking notes, you will *definitely* do better by taking notes. This exam is important. Take it seriously by learning to take notes as you read. Circle the names of characters, underline important moments in the story, and use brief phrases to summarize important ideas about characters and conflicts.

5. The questions are arranged in the order that the story follows. Don't look for answers to the first question in the middle of the story. Chances are you won't be correct.

6. Return to the text as you answer each question. It is right there in front of you, and no one will tell you that you can't look at it once you've read it. The test requires that you go back and reread the text as you answer the questions.

7. Always keep the main idea of the text in mind as you answer the questions. Most of the questions will center on the main idea. Answer choices that stray from the main idea are not usually the correct choices.

8. Read every question carefully. If necessary, write it in your own words in the margin so that you can understand it completely. The job of the test makers is not to make this test easy for you to take. Most

of the time, the test makers will write their questions using complicated phrases and mature vocabulary.

9. Pay attention to the text references and paragraph references in the questions. If a question requires you to look at a certain section of the text, make sure that you return to it. Also, look at the sentences surrounding it. BE CAREFUL. Sometimes, a text reference will require you to focus on only one specific section. At other times, a text reference will lead you to a specific word or phrase, and you will need to determine the context of the question.

10. An answer choice does not need to be incorrect in order for it to be the wrong answer. This will be the first of many tests that you will take in the next four years. You will likely be upset as you review the answers and see you've chosen an answer choice that is partially true. Remember: you have to choose the best option, the one that is totally true, not one that is just partially true. You are right if you think that having partially true options is not fair. Unfortunately, multiple-choice questions require you to choose only one best answer.

11. The test makers are not like your teachers. When your teacher makes up a multiple-choice test, he or she may make the correct answer obvious to those of you who studied. Also, your teacher may even put in one or two goofy multiple-choice options that you would likely never choose. This will NOT happen on the ASK 8 multiple-choice sections. All of the answers will sound reasonable. You will have to determine the correct answer by thinking critically and returning to the text.

PRACTICE READING PASSAGES

To help you prepare for the ASK 8, here are two reading passages, followed by multiple-choice and open-ended questions. They're typical of what appears on the real exam. Follow the instructions and test yourself under timed conditions.

Directions: Read the passage below carefully, taking notes in the margins as you read to ensure comprehension. Then answer the eight multiple-choice questions and open-ended question following each passage.

INFORMATIONAL TEXT (30 MINUTES)

Dancing in the Fast Lane

Over the past ten years, the popularity of Irish step dancing has increased notably. People might attribute this to the renown of *Riverdance* and *Lord of the Dance*. Both shows ran for enthusiastic New York audiences and toured throughout the nation. With such performances in the public eye, many Irish step-dancing schools emerged throughout the country. Irish dancing has changed over the course of the past half century, and more specifically, it has changed in the past two decades. What used to be considered an enjoyable ethnic recreation has turned into a highly competitive sport.

The earliest days of step dancing in America hold cherished memories for many <u>first-generation</u> Irish Americans. These were young men and women whose parents immigrated to the United States from Ireland. As a means of keeping their heritage alive, many parents would contribute part of their hard-earned wages so their sons and daughters could take lessons. These lessons were often quite crowded, held in church halls or school auditoriums. Young students would learn a few steps that they could later dance at parties or family functions. Competitions were minimal, and those who did compete usually did so when the *feis* (competition) was local. Even in those cases, parents could seldom accompany their children because they were working on weekends.

Nothing could be further from this previous scenario these days. Irish step dancers now spend the majority of their spring and summer weekends on the road, covering as many as fifteen competitions in one summer. From coast to coast, each *feis* offers the young dancers the opportunity to gain another medal or trophy. Parents pack up their minivans and load up coolers full of sandwiches and sodas. They set up camp on fairgrounds for the day, complete with folding chairs, tents, radios, and magazines. Because dancers may be in as many as six competitions in one day at any variety of locations, the parents become runners who continually monitor competitions at each stage to make sure their young dancers do not miss their competitions.

Aside from dancing in competition, modern-day Irish step dancers might also perform at various functions, from church dinner dances to political rallies. No St. Patrick's Day parade is complete without step-dancing schools displaying their talent as they march past grandstands and television cameras. Parades and social functions are an excellent way for schools to advertise themselves to the public and gain more students.

In earlier generations, there was no such concept of advertising one's step-dancing school. Word of mouth was the exclusive means of publicizing a step-dancing teacher. At that time, a school consisted of the teacher and his or her students. Nowadays, a school is managed by a teacher who is usually a <u>figurehead</u>, but most of the instructors at step-dancing schools are older students who are accomplished dancers. These students drill the younger students. Instead of taking pay for their work, they receive free lessons themselves.

6   The dancing costume in the 1950s was made up of a basic white shirt, a dark-colored skirt or slacks, and a simple woolen cape pinned to the shoulder. Costumes for competitions today have a starting cost of $900. They are 100 percent wool with intricate Celtic embroidery and satin overlay. Such costumes also require accessories such as rhinestone tiaras and wigs with permanently curled locks. If a modern dancer would like to get the judge's attention in competitions, all of these are suggested. Many parents, disillusioned by the high prices of costumes, try to buy used ones and have them altered. Sometimes, however, this is not acceptable according to certain schools' regulations.

So how has it happened that in a matter of fifty years, the culture of Irish dancing has changed so drastically? Ironically, in their efforts to keep their Irish roots alive in their children, parents have Americanized Irish step dancing. While it was once a simple means of carrying on tradition, step dancing has now become like any other competitive sport in America. Instead of a football camp or a cheerleading workshop, parents are taking their children to a *feis*. Although parents might tell their children that "love of the game" or "love of your culture" is important, they send a different message through their behavior, "Winning IS everything." This is why a significant percentage of step dancers are not Irish at all. They are simply young people who would like to try their hand at a newly emerging competitive sport.

8   Within the world of step dancing, some parents merely want their children to learn a few steps and keep up with family tradition. For these parents, it is more and more difficult to find a school that will accept their needs. Many schools require students to compete throughout the course of the year. They advance students to accelerated classes only once they have placed in a set number of competitions. In brief, students who do not wish to compete are given less instruction than those who do. For this reason, many excellent young dancers leave step dancing to pursue other genres such as jazz, tap, and ballet.

Overall, the culture of Irish dancing has changed over the past half century. It has evolved, as our country has evolved. Step dancing must now keep up with life in the fast lane.

Directions

Circle the correct answer for each question.

1. Which of the following is a reason for the increased popularity of Irish step dancing in America?
   A. its status as a sport
   B. its appeal to people of various cultures
   C. the popularity of *Riverdance* and *Lord of the Dance*
   D. people's increased desire to explore their Irish heritage

2. The purpose of the article is to examine how the general attitude toward Irish step dancing has changed from _____ to _____ .
   A. stressful; peaceful
   B. cultural; competitive
   C. exotic; plain
   D. athletic; artistic

3. The writer uses the term first-generation (paragraph 2) to describe
   A. Irish immigrants.
   B. parents of Irish immigrants.
   C. children of Irish immigrants.
   D. grandchildren of Irish immigrants.

4. What important conclusion does a comparison of the parents described in the second paragraph and the parents described in the third paragraph reveal?
   A. The parents in the second paragraph cared less than the parents in the third paragraph.
   B. The parents in the third paragraph are paying too much attention to their children.
   C. Irish dancing has become more of a family activity.
   D. Both types of parents sacrifice something for their children.

5. Paragraph 6 is best summed up by which of the following statements?
   A. There is a big difference between the dancing costumes of the 1950s and the costumes of today.
   B. Dancers need to stay current with expensive trends to increase their chances of winning.
   C. Only dancers with money can be good dancers.
   D. Irish dancing costumes come with accessories.

6. According to the main idea of the article, which of the following sports could most closely be compared to Irish step dancing?

A. karate

B. swimming

C. track and field

D. yoga

7. What parental challenge does this article summarize?

A. to teach one's children the benefits of competition

B. to emphasize the importance of culture over competition

C. to promote jazz, tap and ballet dancing

D. to pay more attention to their children

8. Considering the author's purpose, the title "Dancing in the Fast Lane" could also be replaced by which of the following titles?

A. "The Benefits of Irish Step Dancing"

B. "Culture Club"

C. "Keeping in Step"

D. "*Lord of the Dance* vs. *Riverdance*"

Directions

Write the answers on a separate sheet of paper. Be sure to write neatly and develop all ideas fully and completely.

9. This article explains how and why Irish dancing has changed.

■ According to the author, in what ways has Irish dancing changed positively?

■ Based on your understanding of the author's opinion, how has Irish dancing changed negatively?

Use evidence from the article to support your answers.

NARRATIVE TEXT (30 MINUTES)

Dinner for Four

By the time she turned thirty, my Aunt Carlota had been married and divorced three times with one child to show for each marriage. I never really knew all the details about why she couldn't stay married. However, I always remember my mother, Carlota's sister, shaking her head each afternoon when Carlota came over to pick up her kids. My mother looked out at Aunt Carlota, who was visibly fatigued.

Aunt Carlota had just come off her shift at the ice cream factory, her second job. Her morning job was at a nursing home. It was against the home's policy to bring kids to work, but Aunt Carlota always signed them in as visitors. My three-year-old cousin Kiki would usually spend the day with Mrs. Holwell. Tony, age eight, would play cards and read with Mr. Neary. Gil would do the rounds with his mother until he found a patient worthy of his four-year-old company.

3 "Why can't Aunt Lottie get a babysitter?" I whined to my mother late one August afternoon. She stood at the kitchen sink, peeling potatoes.

4 "Paolo, do you really want me to answer you again? Now go outside and play with your cousins, or the next time I'll make you stay inside and help me in the kitchen. You know there are always plenty of potatoes that need to be peeled and dishes to be washed." With that, my mother flung the potato peeler into the sink and threw open the back door. I was so glad to get out of there.

5 I hated sharing my backyard with them, hated to see them surfing the channels of our new television, leaving their dirty fingerprints on the screen. I hated how much my mother indulged them. She never corrected them the way she scolded me, and they made mistakes ten times as big as the ones I made. Gil wrote with crayon all over the kitchen wall. My mother just smiled and took a deep breath.

Kiki pooped in the pool. My mother just sighed and went to get the net. Tony would answer my mother back and insult her cooking. Still, my mother would never respond harshly to them. She would never tell Aunt Carlota about any of her children's bad behavior. I asked her why she never told Aunt Lottie about her kids' disrespect.

"What would it change?" my mother said, more a statement than a question.

The only one that Aunt Lottie's kids respected at all was my father. As soon as he came home from work, everyone seemed to stand at attention. I liked how it felt to see their faces tense with fear when they saw him walk through the back gate. He would always kiss me on the top of my head before heading over to his nephews and niece to greet them. He nodded to acknowledge them and then usually asked a question.

"Tony, do you think the butler is coming to pick up that soda can? Put it into the garbage. Why should your Aunt Linda pick up after you? . . . Gil, put that inner tube into the pool shed . . . Kiki, did you wash your hands?"

By the time Aunt Carlota would come to pick up the kids, it was the dinner hour. Most of the time, we would all eat together before Aunt Carlota would take her kids home on the late bus. Because we always had guests, we would never eat in the kitchen. We ate either on the patio or in the basement, the only two places that would have fit all seven of us comfortably. I used to pray for days that Aunt Carlota would get sick and have to stay home. That way, my parents and I would be able to sit at the tiny dinette table in the kitchen and eat a meal in peace.

As I entered my fifth-grade classroom that September, I discovered a miracle. His name was Mr. Jordan. He was a brand new teacher, and he had just moved to Chicago from Peoria. Before he became a teacher, he worked at a bank and went to college at night for eight years. I did the math in my head. That made him 26 at least, maybe older. Aunt Carlota was 32. Who cared? She looked youngish.

That fall, for the first time in my school career, I got straight A's. I was Mr. Jordan's prized pupil. My papers hung from the bulletin boards with gold stars glimmering at their edges. Mr. Jordan's favorite was my composition entitled "Aunt Lottie My Role Model." In the assignment, I wrote all about how hard my Aunt Carlota worked to support her three children, making sure to talk about how beautiful she was and how I hoped she would make a loving wife to someone out there.

12 On Parents' Night, my mother and father were beaming with pride. Mr. Jordan sang my praises and patted me on the shoulder. At that moment, I decided to take my <u>big chance</u>.

"Mr. Jordan should come have dinner at our house one night," I said, smiling up at my parents. "He's new in Chicago."

I looked up at my mother, who smiled awkwardly at Mr. Jordan. She looked over at my father.

"Of course," my father said, clearing his throat and smiling. "Paolo is right. We need to get to know this new teacher who is helping him get such good marks."

I turned and looked at Mr. Jordan, who was turning crimson. "Well," Mr. Jordan said. "That would certainly be nice. I'd love to."

"Great," my mother said. "Friday night at seven?"

18 Aunt Carlota arrived at our house on Friday night at 6:55. She had dark circles under her eyes, and her work pants were torn at the calf. Her hair was falling out of the kerchief she had it tied back in, and she smelled like detergent. Of course, I still thought she was going to be the most beautiful woman in the world to Mr. Jordan, who probably stayed at home every night and graded our papers. Maybe she would go into the bathroom and freshen up a little bit. I waited until she had gone outside to get her kids out of the pool before I asked my mother.

"Mom, did you tell Aunt Lottie that Mr. Jordan was coming over tonight?"

"Of course, Paolo," she replied, turning from the pot of rice on the stove. "It's an important night!"

21 *Wow*, I thought, even my mother knew my plan. Had it been that <u>transparent</u>?

"Well, do you think maybe she could borrow one of your dresses?"

My mother looked perplexed. "Excuse me?"

"You know," I winked, "To meet Mr. Jordan."

"Why would your aunt want to meet Mr. Jordan?" She turned back around to the stove. I looked outside and saw my cousins gathering their things together, heading for the back gate.

"Where are they going?!" I ran to the back door.

"Home, Paolo. They're getting dinner at McDonalds tonight so we can have a nice, quiet dinner with Mr. Jordan. I asked your aunt to take care of dinner for them all tonight." She opened the oven and basted the small roasting chicken.

"But they could stay," I said, "They always stay for dinner."

29 "Paolo, I made enough only for the four of us tonight. They can't stay. Besides, they *should* go out to dinner every once in a while. They should get some time alone as a family."

I ran to the front door and opened it in enough time to see Aunt Carlota trudging down our driveway with all three of her kids in tow. They had reached the foot of the driveway when I called out to her.

"Aunt Carlota!" I yelled across the front lawn. She turned around. Gil was clinging to her leg, Kiki was whining that she was hungry, and Tony was yanking at her arm.

"Yeah, Paolo?"

"Um, are you getting the fish sandwich at McDonalds?"

She shook herself free from Gil's grip. "No, I don't think so."

"Oh, good because it's supposed to have paste in it or something. And the hamburgers are supposed to have horse meat in them."

"Mommy, is it true?" Kiki cried, "I don't want to eat horses!!"

My aunt shot me a dirty look. "Paolo, why on earth would you tell her that?"

The screeching of rubber tires halted our conversation. I looked up to see Mr. Jordan behind the wheel of a tiny Ford Escort. He had just been turning into the driveway when he saw Aunt Carlota and her kids, hit the brakes and stopped, inches short of Tony's legs. Aunt Carlota screamed. Mr. Jordan jumped out of his car.

"I'm so sorry. I didn't see you there. The other car blocked my view as I was turning in."

Aunt Carlota was furious. Her eyes narrowed. "Listen, buddy," she fumed. "You almost hit my son here. Don't you know better than to turn into a driveway like you were getting on the interstate? What are you, stupid or something. Jeez!"

"Ma'am," Mr. Jordan said, looking down. "I am truly sorry for my mistake."

"Well, I would hope you would be." She gathered the kids together one more time and turned down the block, walking behind them like a mother hen.

As Mr. Jordan pulled his car into the driveway, I almost started to cry. Why did she always do that? Was that why she had gotten divorced so much?

I greeted Mr. Jordan as he came up the front walk with a bottle of wine for my parents. *Oh well*, I thought, *there are worse things than good grades.* Then I showed Mr. Jordan into the dining room where my parents waited to have a quiet dinner for four.

Directions

Circle the correct answer for each question.

1. Paolo's question to his mother in paragraph 3 could most logically be answered by which of the following responses?
   A. Aunt Lottie cannot get a babysitter because she'd rather leave her children with a family member.
   B. Aunt Lottie cannot get a babysitter because there is no one available to watch the children during her shift at the ice cream factory.
   C. Aunt Lottie cannot get a babysitter because she does not trust anyone to watch her children properly.
   D. Aunt Lottie cannot get a babysitter because she cannot afford one.

2. Paolo's description of his mother's reaction, "She flung the potato peeler into the sink and threw open the back door" (paragraph 4) shows that his mother feels:
   A. angry at her nephews and niece.
   B. upset with her husband.
   C. frustrated with her son.
   D. furious with her sister.

3. The word <u>indulged</u> (paragraph 5) most nearly means
   A. fed.
   B. spoiled.
   C. excused.
   D. cuddled.

4. Paolo's mother's question, "What would it change?" (paragraph 6) implies what key idea?
   A. Paolo's mother believes that Aunt Carlota would not do anything about her children's bad behavior.
   B. Paolo's mother has tried to change the children's behavior many times.
   C. Paolo's mother believes that Aunt Carlota is a better mother than she is.
   D. Paolo's mother keeps secrets from her sister.

5. The contrast in Paolo's father's behavior around his son (paragraph 7) versus his nephews and niece (paragraph 8) reveals what about his character?
   A. He shows more affection to his son than he does to his niece and nephews.
   B. He is tougher on his niece and nephews because his son is more sensitive.
   C. He feels that Carlota is doing a better job raising her children than he is raising his son.
   D. He treats all the children equally.

6. Paolo's motivation for getting straight A's in school is
   A. to please his parents.
   B. to prove to himself that he can do it.
   C. to overcome his learning disability.
   D. to get his teacher to meet his aunt.

7. The <u>big chance</u> that Paolo mentions (paragraph 12) refers to

   A. his bold invitation to Mr. Jordan that should have come from his parents.

   B. his chance to get straight A's.

   C. his chance to tell Mr. Jordan about his Aunt Lottie.

   D. his chance to have dinner alone with his parents.

8. Paolo's imagined version of Mr. Jordan (paragraph 18) makes an assumption that Mr. Jordan

   A. is a teacher.

   B. is married.

   C. doesn't go out at night.

   D. is uninterested in Aunt Carlota.

9. The word <u>transparent</u> (paragraph 21) most nearly means

   A. obvious.

   B. clear.

   C. mysterious.

   D. fancy.

10. Paolo's mother's statement, "They should get some time alone as a family." (paragraph 29) is ironic because

   A. for the first time, Paolo actually wants his aunt and cousins to stay for dinner.

   B. Aunt Carlota gets plenty of time alone with her family.

   C. Paolo's father has asked for time alone with his family.

   D. Mr. Jordan will not get to meet Aunt Carlota.

Directions

Write the answers to these questions on a separate sheet of paper. Be sure to write neatly and develop all ideas fully and completely.

11. In this story, Paolo offers a picture of his aunt that is not necessarily flattering.

■ Would a boyfriend or husband help or hurt Aunt Lottie's situation?

■ In your opinion, is Aunt Lottie too dependent on other people?

Use details from the story to support your answers.

MULTIPLE-CHOICE ANSWERS AND EXPLANATIONS

Informational Text: "Dancing in the Fast Lane"

1. **C** Although the other answers are mentioned in the article, only option C is referenced.

2. **B** Options A, C, and D might be correct if the words were in reverse order.

3. **C** You should use the context to guide you to the correct answer.

4. **D** This question requires you to exercise your own critical-thinking skills. You will not be able to find the answer to this question in the text itself because the question requires you to draw conclusions from the text and then compare those conclusions. This would be considered a difficult question.

5. **B** Option A and D are both true statements that are mentioned in the article but are not the best responses. Option C is a false conclusion. Option B is correct because it relates specifically to the conclusion that the reader is supposed to draw.

6. **A** When compared with all the other answer choices, karate is the only correct choice because it is a cultural, competitive sport. None of the other options meet these two requirements.

7. **B** Notice the use of the word <u>challenge</u> in the question. Option C is simply a reference to the article. Although options A and D relate to challenges, they do not relate to the specific challenge in the main idea of the article.

8. **C** "Keeping in Step." Option A is incorrect because the essay discusses the effects of Irish dancing, not just the benefits. Option B is too vague, given the content of the essay. Option D addresses something only mentioned in the essay. Only option C touches on the essay's theme.

9. See page 52 for Sample Essay Answer.

Narrative Text: "Dinner for Four"

1. **D** This question requires you to draw a conclusion based on the facts already given in the text. Aunt Carlota takes her children with her to her other job, a clear indicator that she cannot afford a babysitter.

2. **C** Paolo's mother's actions are a reaction to her son's behavior. All of the other options reference different characters' behaviors.

3. **C** All of the behaviors illustrated by Paolo's cousins are excused by his mother. Even though the technical definition of indulge is not to excuse, its connotation in this instance is to excuse.

4. **A** Options B, C, and D are all false statements that cannot be found in the story or inferred by its contents. Only option A can be concluded based on a full reading of the story.

5. **A** Option B is only partially correct. Options C and D can be easily proven wrong by facts in the story. Paolo's father's behavior illustrates the idea in option A.

6. **D** The key word in this question is <u>motivation</u>. In other words, why does Paolo want to get good grades? Although options A and B might sound logical, the facts of the story prove them to be false. Option C is entirely false as there is no indication in the story that Paolo has a learning disability.

7. **A** The question applies to only a certain section of the text. Although option C might seem logical, remember that it was established earlier in the story in Paolo's composition.

8. **C** The key word in this question is <u>assumption</u>. An assumption is a conclusion that is not based on fact and might not be true. As such, options A and B are not possible answers. Option D is not a feasible answer because Mr. Jordan has not yet met Aunt Carlota and, thus far in the story, he has shown some admiration for her.

9. **A** Paolo's mother's statement makes him believe that his intentions have been obvious all along.

10. **A**   The key word in this question is <u>irony</u>, which occurs when the expected outcome differs greatly from the actual outcome. In addition, the line reference here requires you to focus only on the irony of Paolo's mother's statement. Options B and C, although false in the story, do complete ironic statements. Option D also completes a true ironic statement, but it does not relate to Paolo's mother's statement in the line reference.

11.   See page 53 for Sample Essay Answer.

SAMPLE ANSWERS TO OPEN-ENDED QUESTIONS

GETTING A GOOD GRADE ON AN OEQ

An open-ended question, or OEQ, requires you to write a short essay. Don't panic! A short essay is defined as two paragraphs. When you read the OEQ, you should be able to see how the test maker expects you to organize your two paragraphs.

This chapter offers examples of OEQ responses. To get a good grade on your open-ended questions, you have to keep the following tips in mind.

1. Read the OEQs before you read the story. Circle the main idea that the OEQ requires you to write about, and underline references to that main idea in the passage you are reading. This is the best way to find examples to support your answers in your OEQ response. Look at the sample OEQ below:

The author of this article identifies challenges and successes that teachers experience every day.

■ Identify one challenge experienced by a teacher in the article. How does the teacher overcome it?
■ Identify one success achieved by a teacher in the article. How does the teacher achieve it?

Use evidence from the article to support and develop your answer.

This question provides you with a road map for reading the story. As you read, you should focus on challenges and successes. Look at the sample below to see what a marked-up passage should look like:

<table>
<tr><td>*challenge</td></tr>
</table>

<table>
<tr><td>*success</td></tr>
</table>

<table>
<tr><td>*challenge</td></tr>
</table>

<table>
<tr><td>*success</td></tr>
</table>

<table>
<tr><td>*challenge/success</td></tr>
</table>

In this film, the main character, Jaime Escalante, teaches an advanced-level mathematics class to unmotivated urban students. Mr. Escalante must use a variety of unique teaching strategies in order to get his students to achieve higher goals. He also has to look very closely at the factors that keep his students from succeeding and help them each believe in themselves. When the students' exam scores reflect exceptional excellence, Mr. Escalante is questioned by the test makers and his administration. People cannot believe that students who had been so mediocre prior to his class might perform so well in such a short period of time. The way that Mr. Escalante and his students respond to this injustice illustrates how they have truly learned from their experiences.

As you read, you should make note of the main ideas posed in the OEQs. That way, you will be at an advantage when it comes time to write your response. You will also know exactly where to go in the text to find support for your answers. Do not be afraid to write on your text or to mark it up. This is an excellent test-taking strategy that you should get used to now.

2. All OEQs will actually bullet point two or more separate questions for you to answer within one OEQ response. Each bullet-pointed question should receive a one-paragraph response.

3. Each paragraph in your OEQ response should have a clear topic sentence. A topic sentence states what will be proven in the paragraph.

To make a good topic sentence, look back at the question and flip it around, adding your point. For example:

Question: Identify one success achieved by a teacher in the article. How does the teacher achieve it?

Answer: One challenge that Mr. Escalante must face is his students' lack of motivation, which he helps them to overcome by getting his students to believe in themselves.

Be sure to stay focused on what the topic sentence claims you are proving. In this case, clear examples of and reasons for students' lack of motivation should be mentioned throughout the paragraph.

4. Each of the paragraphs in the OEQ response should contain two to three examples from the reading passage. Details from the text make a good score! In general, one example per paragraph should be quoted from the reading passage. *Note: Any sentence that you take from the text has to be enclosed within quotes to show that it is not your writing.* The quoted example should be incorporated into your sentence as smoothly as possible. Try not to let quotations stand alone unless they are really great. Here is an example of a well-incorporated quote:

> One reason that the students lack motivation is the fact that no one believes in them. Even when they do succeed, they are considered "mediocre" students because of their past school records.

A quotation need not be long to be effective. However, be sure to select a key word or phrase if your quotation is shorter.

5. Avoid using slang, clichés, and colloquialisms. These are all terms that describe words or phrases that are more often heard on the street than written in a formal essay. (Examples include "totally awesome," "so messed up," and "don't judge a book by its cover.") They are overused. Your own ideas matter more to the reader.

6. Write in the present tense. If you stay in the present tense, you won't have to worry about switching too

much. The present tense is the easiest to write in because it is the least wordy and the most focused.

For example, do not write, "Courage is demonstrated by the main character when he went to the store and had returned the candy he had stolen earlier that week." This is too wordy. The present tense is shorter and more concise. It would read, "The main character's courage is evident when he revisits the store and returns the stolen candy."

If your quotations are in the past tense, don't change them. Just keep all of your own words in present tense as much as possible.

7. Use mature vocabulary. Your teachers do vocabulary exercises with you for a reason. They want you to use those words in your speech and writing. Now is your golden opportunity. The readers will reward you for what you do well. Even if the word isn't quite right, chances are they'll reward your effort for trying to use it.

8. Remember to write all your answers as full sentences, with appropriate capitalization, punctuation, and grammar. This rule may seem basic, but many students write as if they are texting. This is formal writing! Make sure your writing looks its best!

SAMPLE ANSWERS AND SCORES

This chapter corresponds to the narrative and informational text exercises you did in Chapter 4. In the appendix of this book is the rubric for scoring the open-ended questions. Remember, an easy way to think of the scoring is like this:

4 = A   3 = B   2 = C   1 = D/F

You should have written answers to the open-ended questions on a separate sheet of paper. In this chapter, you will have the opportunity to compare the answers you have written to some sample answers offered. You never know when some of the suggestions you read might help you in the future!

Sample Question and Response for "Dancing in the Fast Lane"

This article claims that the change in Irish dancing is also related to cultural changes.

■ How have parents of Irish dancers changed?
■ How has the level of competition changed?

Use evidence from the article to support your answers.

One element of Irish dancing that has changed is the attitude of dancers' parents. They have become more involved than the parents in previous generations. Parents are focusing more on the competitive elements of Irish dancing than they are on the cultural elements of it. It has become "Americanized" because parents are much more involved. "Parents become runners" who are highly involved in their children's activities. They send the message to their kids that "winning IS everything." Parents' attitudes have changed from easygoing to high intensity.

Another aspect of Irish dancing that has changed is the level of competition. Irish dancing contests used to be only local, but now they are long distance. Dancers participate in "as many as fifteen competitions in one summer." This compares to only a few for dancers years ago. In addition, the competition costumes have become very expensive and fancy. If a dancer wants to win, she has to have the best costume and the best dance steps. Clearly, the level of competition has increased.

Score for sample answer: 3

What does the writer do well?

■ Uses clear topic sentences and clear closing sentences.
■ Incorporates quotations into the paragraphs.
■ Uses clear examples to support the ideas.

What could the writer do to get a score of 4?

■ Use more transitions in the first paragraph. All of the sentences begin with either a noun or a pronoun.

■ Choose a better quote to use in the second paragraph. The information in the quote is not so interesting that it has to be quoted. It could be paraphrased.

Sample Response for "Dinner for Four"

11. In this story, Paolo offers a picture of his aunt that is not necessarily flattering.

■ Would a boyfriend or husband help or hurt Aunt Lottie's situation?

■ In your opinion, is Aunt Lottie too dependent on other people?

Use details from the story to support your answers.

Getting a new husband would definitely not help Aunt Lottie's situation. Firstly, she has already been "divorced three times with one child to show for each marriage." It would definitely take a lot for any guy to marry a woman who already had three children. Chances are he would have a few of his own, and Aunt Lottie already can't handle the ones she has. Also, if she had one child with each of her husbands, she might have a child with her next husband. Any man would be crazy to marry Aunt Lottie because she's moody and mean.

A second reason that Aunt Lottie should not date or get married is that she will get into the habit of depending on a man. Obviously, she got into that habit before, and it got her into the trouble she's in now. It is true that her kids want a father figure. Paolo's father is "the only one that Aunt Lottie's kids respected." Unfortunately, Aunt Lottie has depended on too many other people to raise her children for her, and she thinks her children are a burden that should be lifted from her. When she is seen "trudging" down the block with her children, it is clear that she wants a break. However, a man will not be able to give her a break.

Score for sample answer: 2

Reasons for the score:

■ Both of the paragraphs need better closure.
■ The writer should not use words like "guy," "crazy," and "kids."
■ The second quotation in the second paragraph is not relevant and should be replaced with a better example.

CHAPTER SUMMARY

Practicing answering the open-ended questions and seeing a variety of responses should help you understand what constitutes a strong response.

Keep these things in mind for good OEQ responses:

■ Read the questions first. Then mark the text by underlining as you read.
■ Write a clear topic sentence by flipping the question into a statement.
■ Back up the topic sentence with evidence from the text. Include quotes from the text and draw comparisons from your own life.
■ Write clear sentences that include proper punctuation, capitalization, and grammar. Mechanics are an important part of the score!
■ Write in the present tense; avoid informal vocabulary.

Because you are working under timed conditions, you have to practice writing responses to open-ended questions during restricted time. If you practice enough, you will be comfortable by the time the test is given!

WRITING THE PERSUASIVE ESSAY

KEY POINTS TO REMEMBER

You'll hear this a lot in high school: *"Every piece of writing has a purpose and an audience."* This is true, but a lot of students forget it over time. If you are writing a newspaper article, what is your purpose? You want to inform people about what has happened recently. If you are writing a recipe, who is your audience? You hope that someone who likes to cook will read your writing. So let's think about your task on the ASK 8.

> Note: What if your essay is the first one of the day? What if it is the last one? What if your essay comes after the best one the reader has looked at all day? These are all possibilities, so do your best at all times.

- What is the purpose of the persuasive essay? You want to *persuade* the reader that your point is correct.
- Who is the audience? Individuals who will be reading *hundreds* of essays on the *same* topic over a *short* period is your audience.

Imagine a room full of adults, all of whom have to read hundreds of essays in a short period of time. How might these people differ from your English/language arts teacher?

1. They don't have the time to write notes on your essay the way your teacher does.
2. They've never met you, and they don't know you the way your teacher does.
3. They're likely not going to "cut you a break" the way your teacher sometimes does if you do poorly on an assignment because you lost a game yesterday or had a fight with your brother this morning.

4. They read your work once and score it based on first impression. Keep in mind the scoring rubric, located in the appendix of this book. Once again, an easy way to think of it is:

6 = A+
5 = A
4 = B
3 = C
2 = D
1 = F

HOW TO PREPARE

ORGANIZATION, ORGANIZATION, ORGANIZATION!!!! Your persuasive essay must consist of five paragraphs, with an introduction (including a clear statement of your thesis), three supporting paragraphs, and a conclusion.

What Is a Thesis?

You hear people use the word *thesis* all the time, but what does it mean? Are a thesis and a topic sentence the same thing? No. They are related, though. Let's take this one step at a time. When you are given an essay prompt on the ASK 8, there is always a hint about what your thesis might be.

What Is an Essay Prompt?

An essay prompt is the *situation* and *set of directions* that you are given to write the persuasive essay. It provides all background information needed to write your persuasive essay. Look at this example:

It is January during midterm exams at your school when a fire alarm sounds. The entire building is evacuated immediately in the freezing temperatures, and the fire department does not arrive for twenty minutes, making it clear that this was not a planned fire drill. As everyone files back into school, many students complain that this isn't fair. They've lost thirty minutes off their seventy-five minute exam period. Several students ask their teachers what they should do, and teachers advise their students to do the best they can in the time remaining. At the end of the exam period, Principal Hart's voice sounds on the public address system. He tells all of the students that the alarm was pulled as a prank. He then says that unless someone reports the prankster by the beginning of the school day tomorrow, students will not be granted extra time on their exams.

Write a letter to your principal explaining why you do or do not support his disciplinary strategy. Give clear reasons for your support or criticism of his ultimatum to the students of your school. Use the space on the next page to brainstorm and prewrite an outline.

Note: Remember that "letter" means essay. A letter has a purpose and an audience. How would you go about answering this essay prompt?

What Are Brainstorming and Prewriting?

Brainstorming is jotting down a list of important ideas or making a web or mind map of ideas related to your topic. This gets you thinking about how you're going to organize yourself.

Prewriting is outlining your ideas and organizing them into an introduction, a body, and a conclusion.

Lots of people skip these steps, and that is not a wise idea. You should definitely take the time to brainstorm and prewrite. If you do, your essay will be better organized. You won't forget to include any important, persuasive arguments. In addition, your points will be presented in a logical manner. Chances are that you will receive a higher score than if you didn't brainstorm and prewrite.

And, believe it or not, you will finish the essay faster if you make an outline first! Making a plan and following it takes less time than constantly having to stop and think about what you want to say next. Brainstorming and outlining will get you better scores in less time! It's a win-win strategy!

AN EASY WAY TO BRAINSTORM

Draw a line down the prewriting page. Put "For" on one side and "Against" on the other. Now think of the topic and jot down ideas as they come to mind.

Note: Try to think of ideas that are unusual! Coming up with ideas that are different from other people's will set your essay apart!

For example:

For	Against
■ The prankster disrupted everyone and should be punished.	■ It's not fair for students to focus on this when they should be studying.
■ Turning the prankster in will show the school that students are responsible.	■ Snitching puts us in a dilemma.
	■ Person accused might not be the prankster.

If you're stuck brainstorming, there are three topics that can almost always be turned into ideas:

1. Money. For example: The prankster should be turned in because he cost the fire department money for gas and manpower to respond to the false alarm, in addition to the expense of the investigation.
2. Family. For example: Family plans (practice for sports or possibly a special occasion such as a dinner out or a birthday celebration) have to be changed now that students must spend another night studying.
3. Safety. For example: What if there had been a real fire emergency in town? With the fire department responding to the school alarm, people in jeopardy might have been without help.

Now give prewriting for this topic a try on the next page.

Prewriting/Planning Space

Did you use the space provided to brainstorm and pre-write your own ideas? If not, go back and do it. If you have, pay close attention to the terms below—thesis, hook, and central idea—which only apply after you have jotted down some ideas.

AFTER BRAINSTORMING

Once you've spent three or four minutes brainstorming ideas, look at what you have. What side will make a better essay? In this example, the Against side will be a better essay, and so the For side will be discarded.

If you only have two reasons, you don't have a good persuasive essay! You should always include three examples to make your argument. You have probably heard people say, "Give me three good reasons why . . ." This is a common method of organization in writing and in life. When you make an argument as you are doing in the persuasive essay, it takes three reasons to really pack a punch. One or two are just not enough.

THE THESIS

Once you have completed the brainstorming, the next step is to write the thesis, which is the point you're trying to prove in your essay. Think of it like a topic sentence for the whole essay.

Here is a formula that every thesis has:

The Topic + Your Opinion = Thesis Statement

Some people include the reasons in the thesis statement. If you do, make sure that you put them in the order in which they will appear.

Note: Generally, don't use "I" or "me" or "my"—as in "I think that . . ." The thesis statement is about the topic, not about you.

For example, here are three thesis statements for the topic:

- Mr. Hart, you should not make the prankster confess.
  OR
- Mr. Hart, you should not make students turn in the prankster because it puts students in a dilemma, it might not be the actual prankster, and it takes the focus off studying for exams.
  OR
- Mr. Hart, you are doing the right thing because the person should be punished, the prank interfered with exams, and everyone should help find the person who did this.

 The thesis should never be the very first sentence of a persuasive essay/letter.

Don't ever write the thesis as your first sentence. Whether you are writing an essay or a letter, you have to take the following approach. Start with a good hook. Then branch into your central idea. Finally, state your thesis at the end of the introduction.

PUTTING IT TOGETHER

Once you've brainstormed ideas and written your thesis statement, the next step is to organize your ideas. In a persuasive essay, use order of importance for your ideas. Order of importance puts your reasons in order from weakest to strongest. People always expect an essay to get better as it goes; so if you don't end with your best, the reader will be let down (and that, of course, will affect your score).

Look back at your best three reasons. The weakest will be paragraph two, the middle, paragraph three, and the strongest, paragraph four. Add any supporting details you can think of.

Here's an example:

Against
- Snitching puts us in a dilemma.
- Person accused might not be the prankster.
- It's not fair for students to focus on this when they should be studying.

Paragraph 1 will be the intro, ending with the thesis statement. Here is a quick plan for an introduction outline:

- Hook
- Central Idea
- Thesis

Paragraph 5 will be the conclusion. Here is a simple way to plan a conclusion:

- <u>Restate</u> (don't copy) the thesis statement.

For example: I am opposed to your strategy of snitching.

- Summarize the first reason (paragraph 2)
- Summarize the second reason (paragraph 3)
- Summarize the third reason (paragraph 4)
- End with a strong closing statement (Demand what you want!)

For example: I sincerely hope you change your disciplinary style.

THE INTRODUCTION/HOOK

A hook is a general idea that is well phrased and gets people interested in reading more. Some examples of good hooks include:

- A famous quote
- A statistic
- A shocking statement
- A greeting (in the case of the prompt requiring you to write a letter)
- A question

For example, a good hook for this topic would be:

Dear Principal Hart,

 Should law-abiding students be punished for the negligence of one bad student? I am writing to share my opinion with you about the recent fire drill issue.

Why is this a good hook?

1. It is a question that already implies the opinion of the writer.
2. It introduces the general topic.
3. It can then be followed by information learned from the prompt and details to support the writer's position.

THE CENTRAL IDEA

The central idea is related to the general idea, but it is more specific. The central idea links the hook together with the thesis. In this case, use information from the prompt to be more specific. Here is an example of an effective general idea:

 Even though I know that the guilty student must be punished, I don't believe that the approach you are taking is fair.

FINAL RESULT

Dear Principal Hart,

Should law-abiding students be punished for the negligence of one bad student? I am writing to share my opinion with you about the recent fire drill issue. Even though I know that the guilty student must be punished, I don't believe that the approach you are taking is fair. Mr. Hart, you should not make students turn in the prankster because it puts students in a dilemma, it might not be the actual prankster, and it takes the focus away from studying for exams.

Your introduction paragraph is a road map for the rest of your essay. What does that mean? Well, by looking at your introduction, your reader should see exactly where you are going to go in the essay. This introduction makes it very clear to the reader what the next three body paragraphs are about. Can you see what the three body paragraph topics are going to be about?

1. Putting students in a dilemma
2. Possibly not finding the actual prankster
3. Taking the focus off exams

Each of these reasons supports your thesis. Each one will be discussed in a separate paragraph with a separate topic sentence, and they will be written in the same order.

Body Paragraphs

The body paragraphs all support the thesis statement. Remember, you must be <u>for</u> or <u>against</u> the dilemma. If you try to write an essay that's a little bit for and a little bit against, you will look like you don't know. If you look like you don't know, you will not get a good score. The body paragraph is made up of the topic sentence, supporting details, and the clincher (concluding) sentence.

The Topic Sentence

A topic sentence is the first sentence of a body paragraph, and it differs from your thesis. A topic sentence represents one of the three supporting ideas in your thesis. It must be supported by three more examples or pieces of evidence in the body paragraph. Look below at each of the three topic sentences. What do you notice?

- Firstly, Mr. Hart, by asking us to snitch on a classmate, you are putting us in a social dilemma.
- In addition to my first point, consider that the person accused might not be the prankster at all.
- Lastly, it is not fair to have students focus on this problem when we should be studying for our exams.

Each one of these topic sentences introduces the main idea of the paragraph. In addition, each one uses a transitional word or phrase to establish where the paragraph is placed in the essay.

Transitional Words and Phrases

A transitional word or phrase is a tool that the writer uses to help show the reader where he or she is going. For example, you have likely been taught that when you write a conclusion, you use the words *in conclusion* to start off your body paragraph. There are lots of other transitional words and phrases to use in a conclusion: *to close, to sum up, to reflect,* and *finally* are some good ones.

However, transitional words should be used throughout your essay, and especially in your topic sentences. Notice that the words "Firstly," "In addition," and "Lastly" establish each of your three examples. The introductory paragraph includes the phrase "even though." How is this different from "Firstly," "In addition," and "Lastly"? Well, "even though" indicates that there are two opposing ideas. In this case, the idea of the principal and the idea of the student. Below is a basic list of transitional phrases to use. Get into the habit of using them in your persuasive writing, and make sure to ask your teacher if you are using them correctly.

Transitional phrases that show organization:

To begin with
Firstly/secondly/thirdly
Finally
In addition
Also
Another example of this

Transitional phrases that show opposing ideas:

Even though
While
Although
In spite of the fact that
On the other hand

Transitional phrases that criticize an idea:

Nonetheless
Nevertheless
Regardless of
Instead

Transitional phrases that offer closure or reinforcement:

Clearly
As it has been proven
Evidently
Truly
In fact
For all of these reasons
Undoubtedly
Unquestionably

Supporting Details

Giving only a reason is not enough to convince a reader of your idea; therefore, your essay will fail to reach its goal. You must back up those reasons with supporting details. Supporting details can be

- facts
- examples
- statistics (number facts)
- anecdotes (brief stories that you know)

Note: If you use facts or statistics, you cannot just make them up. Outside of the obvious problem of plagiarism and lying, made-up facts almost always <u>sound</u> made up. Remember, the people who score these essays read one after another. They quickly learn to recognize when a student is faking it.

The Clincher (Concluding) Sentence

The clincher (sometimes called concluding) sentence is similar to the topic sentence. However, where the topic sentence <u>introduces</u> your reason, your clincher sentence <u>wraps</u> up your reason. If you're having trouble getting started on your clincher, look back to the topic sentence for the main idea. Then ask yourself, "How would I sum up that reason?"

ESSAY PRACTICE EXERCISE

On the next page there's a series of blanks for the essay, but only a topic sentence is provided for each paragraph. You are to complete each paragraph, using at least three transitional words or phrases from the lists on page 66 in each of your three paragraphs. You may repeat some, but try to use a variety of them.

Firstly, Mr. Hart, by asking us to snitch on a classmate, you are putting us in a social dilemma.

_____

_____

_____

_____

_____

_____

_____

_____

_____

_____

_____

In addition to my first point, consider that the person accused might not be the prankster at all.

_____

_____

_____

_____

_____

_____

_____

_____

_____

_____

_____

Lastly, it is not fair to have students focus on this problem when we should be studying for our exams.

_____

_____

_____

_____

_____

_____

_____

_____

_____

_____

_____

Now that you have had some time to practice, look at the three sample body paragraphs that follow. Mark every transitional word or phrase.

Firstly, Mr. Hart, by asking us to snitch on a classmate, you are putting us in a social dilemma. As far as I know, the person who pulled the alarm is not a friend of mine. If it was, however, I don't think I would be able to tell on him or her. A true friend is a person who can forgive someone's mistakes. A real friend would give up the good grade to protect his friend from getting punished. Also, let's be realistic. Who would really want to tell on someone to the principal? I'd lose all my friends if I did that.

In addition to my first point, consider that the person accused might not be the prankster at all. In fact, wouldn't it be possible for someone to lie and get someone else in trouble? Suppose I had just had a fight with my friend this morning and decided to report him as the prankster. You would get the name of the person, but it wouldn't be the truth. A situation like this gives people the opportunity to cause trouble instead of solving the problem.

Lastly, it is not fair to have students focus on this problem when we should be studying for our exams. Now, everyone will be on Facebook tonight talking about how unfair all of this is. Instead of studying, we'll all be complaining about how unfair this is. As a result, everyone will do poorly on two exams instead of just one. Your idea puts more pressure on us when we're already stressed enough.

Do you see any similarities between your paragraphs and these sample ones? How are they similar? How are they different? Most importantly, <u>did you back up the reasons with supporting details</u>?

THE ALL-IMPORTANT CONCLUSION

Most people don't like writing a conclusion. Many students say it is repetitive. However, a good conclusion will do three things:

1. Restate the thesis (do not copy and paste) by restating your opinion and summarizing your reasons.
2. Put closure on the essay by reinforcing your point.
3. End with a strong closing statement.

If you plan the conclusion before writing, as we did in the outline, it is far easier to write. Look at the plan again:

A. <u>Restate</u> (don't copy) the thesis statement.

> *For example: I am opposed to your strategy of snitching.*

B. Summarize the first reason (paragraph 2).
C. Summarize the second reason (paragraph 3).
D. Summarize the third reason (paragraph 4).
E. End with a strong closing statement (Demand what you want!).

> *For example: I sincerely hope you change your disciplinary style.*

Now look at the example below:

Clearly, you can see that I am opposed to your strategy for finding out who pulled the fire alarm. It puts us in a social dilemma, it opens the door to more potential mischief, and it makes us focus on the wrong thing during an important time. For all of these reasons, I sincerely hope that you reconsider your disciplinary style.

Now that you have a clear idea of how to organize the persuasive essay, you are going to try writing an essay on your own.

_____

_____

_____

_____

_____

_____

_____

_____

_____

_____

_____

_____

_____

_____

_____

_____

_____

_____

_____

_____

Now it's time to do some more practice exercises. On the pages that follow, you will see four practice essay prompts. Use the white space below each prompt to brainstorm, web, or outline the ideas for your essay. Following each of the prompts will be an example essay that responds to the prompt. You should consider these essays to be model essays that would receive scores of a 5 or 6. Look very closely at how they are organized and what the writer does well. Keep the scoring rubric located in the appendix of this book in mind as you write your essay and read the sample essays.

Essay Prompt #1

Recently, a student in your school was suspended for carrying a knife in his backpack. The knife was discovered when he left the back pocket open during class and a teacher saw it sticking out of the bag. As a result of this event, your school's administrators are considering doing spot checks of backpacks and lockers periodically. They believe that these spot checks will ensure school safety.

Write a letter to your principal explaining why you do or do not support the practice of randomly spot-checking backpacks and lockers. Give clear reasons for your support or criticism of this possible school policy. Make sure to develop each of your reasons fully and completely. You have 45 minutes to complete this essay.

Prewriting/Planning Space

Prewriting/Planning Space

Model Essay for Prompt #1

Dear Principal,

Would you please open up your purse and show me everything that's inside it? I'd like to see if there's anything in there that might make me suspect that you are a criminal. How did it make you feel to be asked that question? You can definitely imagine how it makes me feel knowing that I could come to school every day and have my personal things rifled through by someone I really don't know. I disagree with the policy you are proposing, because I believe it is an invasion of privacy. In addition, the policy will also cause profiling in the school. Lastly, the policy does not give the student the benefit of the doubt.

This policy is an invasion of privacy. At home, my parents trust me to finish my homework, remember my lunch, and do a lot of other things that don't require their constant supervision. I follow their rules because I respect them as my parents. In the same way, I follow your rules because I respect you as my principal. If you do a good job, then you shouldn't have to worry about me breaking the rules.

Another reason why I strongly disagree with this policy is that it will cause profiling. Even in the subways of New York City, people say that they feel profiling exists during bag checks. If the police do it, then so can you. Let's suppose that I have a friend who has a decal for the band The Killers on his backpack. Will you assume when you see that decal that my friend is a violent person? Will the kids with tie-dyed backpacks be considered hippies? Will you suspect that they do drugs? Just because a student might look a certain way or dress a certain way doesn't mean that the student behaves like that stereotype.

Thirdly, this policy does not give the students the benefit of the doubt. If we are supposed to feel safe in schools, doesn't safety start with trust? If I carry a water gun in my backpack, it may be for a skit I'm doing for drama class. If I have a picture of marijuana in my locker, it might be for a project I'm doing for science class. That can of spray paint you see in the

*This hook would be considered a successful compositional risk. It grabs the reader's attention and draws the reader into the argument right away.

*The thesis is very clear, and the organization is evident:
1. Invasion of privacy
2. Causes profiling
3. No benefit of the doubt
This is a great roadmap for the reader!

*Logical progression of ideas and a good transition from one idea to the next.

*Offering hypothetical situations is an effective persuasive strategy to convince the reader.

*This writer uses RHETORICAL QUESTIONS throughout the essay. These are questions that already imply the answer and reveal the writer's stance on the topic.

*Your closure need not be long, but make sure that it is evident. Only essays with both opening and closure will score a 6 on the rubric.

side pocket of my backpack is going to get used after school when we make signs for the car wash. Could I really get suspended for being a good student and a model school citizen? It's possible if these spot checks are permitted.

As a final reflection, I will offer you this thought. Teachers are always telling us not to "judge a book by its cover." If you allow this policy to be in effect, this will be the very practice that you promote. Thank you for taking the time to read my letter, and I hope that you will definitely consider my point of view.

Sincerely,
John Q. Student

Essay Prompt #2

Over the course of the next three years, your school building will be undergoing major construction and renovation. This will require hundreds of hours of construction that must be done during the day as well as on the weekends. As a result, your district must change the daily school schedule. Right now, the Board of Education is considering two possible school day schedules. Schedule *A* would require students to be in school from 8:00 A.M. until 2:00 P.M. from August until June. Schedule *B* would require students to be in school from 8:00 A.M. until 4:00 P.M. from October through May.

The Board of Education is requiring every student in the district to write an essay in his or her English class. The essay must argue for one of the two schedules. Write your essay, giving clear reasons for your support of either schedule *A* or schedule *B*. Make sure to develop each of your reasons fully and completely. You have 45 minutes to complete this essay.

Prewriting/Planning Space

Prewriting/Planning Space

Model Essay for Prompt #2

*Consider using a brief personal narrative in your introduction. It interests the reader right away.

*By using transitional words like "firstly," secondly," and "finally," the writer guides the reader through the thesis statement.

*It is all right to use "statistic" in your essay. Even if it is not exact, you are still showing effort to prove your point.

*Throughout this paragraph and the essay as a whole, the writer uses a cause and effect strategy. The writer uses various forms of if . . . then statements to illustrate how schedule *A* would be effective.

How many hours did you sleep last night? I got about five, and that was a pretty high number for me. By the time I get home from soccer practice, eat dinner, and get all my homework done, it's usually about 12:30 or 1:00 A.M. In the morning, if I want to get to the shower before my sister, I have to be up at 6:00 to have the bathroom to myself. As you can see, I would be in favor of schedule A. There are three reasons that I would support schedule A. Firstly, it would give me the opportunity to sleep more. Secondly, it would strengthen the athletic programs. Finally, it would give me more time to study.

Right now, the school day starts at 7:15. If the school day started at 8:00, I would have more time to sleep. Statistics show that students between the ages of twelve and eighteen need at least eight hours of sleep per night. Nobody I know sleeps more than five or six hours at the most. This is because schedules are packed so tightly that there is no time to sleep. More sleep equals better brain functioning. If I had eight hours of sleep per night, I would definitely be a better student. It would definitely improve the quality of my life.

I love being on the soccer team, but during soccer season my grades usually go down a little bit. This is because we usually have practice and games until very late and there is no time for me to do my homework as well as I can. However, if the school day ended at 2:00, I could get a lot of work done before practice at 4:00. Even if we had a game, there would still be extra time to get work done because other schools don't have our schedule. Also, if the team needed more time to practice, we wouldn't have to go later—we could just start earlier! It would definitely improve morale on our team.

Schedule A would also give me more time to study. It is always difficult working on a group project after school. With Schedule A, though, it wouldn't be hard at all. My group could get together and work on a project with no conflict. In addition, if I wanted to have a friend tutor me or go to a teacher for extra help, it wouldn't be a time conflict. All in all, schedule

*This writer is not afraid to acknowledge the negative side of schedule *A*, because the entire essay has developed why schedule *A* is so positive.

*Notice that this is not an exact copy and paste of the thesis statement. Think about how you can rephrase your thesis so that it does not sound too repetitive.

*The essay is best concluded with a powerful, thought-provoking comment.

A offers me a lot of flexibility and choice in what to do with my time. Even though it is over the course of eleven months, I would still prefer it, because a month for vacation is plenty of time. We would also get regular vacations during the school year, too.

   To sum up, I support schedule A, because I believe it is the best schedule for students my age. It focuses on what's important to us: sleep, sports, and reducing academic stress. I fully support schedule A and hope that the board votes for it. If schedule A does not come to pass, then I certainly hope that the board is ready to deal with the consequences: cranky, strung-out students with no hope of a winning season.

Essay Prompt #3

A recent news report in a neighboring town states that police have arrested and detained three youths for gang activity. The three youths were all wearing red hats that identify them as members of the same gang. In fact, many gang members identify themselves by their headgear in local malls and other town hangouts. As a result of this recent event, county police are asking school districts to reevaluate their current policy on headgear.

Your school is considering banning all headgear for boys and girls. This ban would include hats, visors, do-rags, bandannas, and headbands. This will be voted on by your student council at its next meeting. Your English teacher has assigned your class to write a five-paragraph essay arguing for or against the banning of headgear. The student council representative in your English class will read the best essay aloud at the meeting before the voting takes place. Write your essay, arguing for or against this ban. Give clear reasons for your viewpoint, and make sure to develop each of your reasons fully and completely. You have 45 minutes to complete this essay.

Prewriting/Planning Space

Prewriting/Planning Space

Model Essay for Prompt #3

Anyone who supports the ban on headgear has clearly lost his or her head. The fact that this rule is even being considered is ludicrous. Headgear should not be banned in our school but embraced. Headgear shows a person's beliefs and values. In addition, it covers bad hair that no one wants to see. Finally, headgear can be worn for more personal reasons that are nobody's business.

Hats, bandannas, and do-rags aren't just accessories that are worn by shallow people. They show the values and beliefs of a person. If a student is Jewish and wants to wear a yarmulke, no rule should prevent that student from doing so. Another student may have had a mother who died of breast cancer. If that student wants to wear a pink breast cancer bandanna, she should be able to! Hats can show others so much about a person, from the baseball team one loves to the university one wants to attend.

Have you ever had a bad hair day? I know I have. If I couldn't wear a hat, I would be miserable. Everyone has those days when they need to wear a hat or cover up their hair in some way. Suppose I got a bad haircut or made the mistake of dying my hair purple. Do I have to show my horrible hairdo to everyone? Have some compassion. If you've ever overslept and not had the chance to wash your hair, a hat makes all the difference. There are other mornings when there's just no time to do your hair the way you want it.

Finally, consider that some people might take refuge in wearing a hat for personal reasons. There's one boy in my math class who is painfully shy. His hat is like his refuge. When he wears it, he doesn't have to look someone in the eye. Another friend of mine has terrible acne around her forehead. Some days, she really just needs to wear a headband. Will the headgear rule apply to students who have cancer and are undergoing chemotherapy?

---

*Plays on words are always good tools to use for both hooks and conclusions. In this case, the writer uses the word *head* in a fun way.

*Each of these situations presents an emotional appeal to the reader. The writer presents a variety of sensitive, personal reasons for wearing hats.

*Statements like this help to put the reader into someone else's shoes, which is an effective persuasive technique.

*This is an effective use of a simile. It is a vivid use of language and will catch the reader's attention.

*Although this might seem a little dramatic, it is the type of compositional risk that will be rewarded.

In addition to having cancer, will those students have to deal with the ridicule of being called names like eight ball? All of these points should be considered before making any kind of decision across the board.

We are taught in school to be ourselves and stand up for what we believe in. If the headgear ban goes into effect, it will go against everything we've been taught. Please do not vote for the headgear ban. It will drastically change our school and our lives.

Essay Prompt #4

Today in your physical education class, your teacher asks you not to get changed. She hands out a copy of a recent article to your class and reads it out loud. The article is about the P.E. program in your neighboring state. The program offers students the opportunity to take honors level P.E. Students who take honors level P.E. get more academic credits than other students who take regular level P.E. This can help bring up their grade point averages. According to the article, honors level P.E. is popular with many students and especially those students who are less "academically" talented.

Your P.E. teacher wants to know your opinion on this topic. She hands out paper and assigns the class to write an essay that supports or challenges the idea of an honors level P.E. class. Write your essay, arguing for or against this program. Give clear reasons for your viewpoint, and make sure to develop each of your reasons fully and completely. You have 45 minutes to complete this essay.

Prewriting/Planning Space

Prewriting/Planning Space

Model Essay for Prompt #4

Everyone has talents that should be rewarded. For students who are athletically talented, however, the reward is not always academic. Of course, teams can have wonderful seasons, but when is a student academically rewarded for being a good athlete? Offering an honors level physical education class is a great idea. It would make students take P.E. more seriously, put students in a competitive group, and offer the academic reward that they deserve.

*This writer is able to get the thesis into one sentence by organizing the argument into three verbs:
1. make students take seriously
2. put in group
3. offer reward

A lot of students do not take P.E. seriously. They consider it an "easy" class because all you have to do is play. Some students even think that they can use their P.E. period to make up a test or quiz, because "it's just gym." If P.E. was given honors level credit, students would take it a lot more seriously. They would remember to bring their gym uniforms every day, and they wouldn't be late.

Another reason why honors level P.E. is a great idea is that it groups great athletes together. As a result, the games are much more competitive. Each student would play to his or her best ability instead of lowering the level of competition to suit the weaker players. The teacher could also take more time to focus on specific skills with the students instead of just a general understanding of games. By the end of the year, the students in honors level P.E. would have improved physically as a result of taking the class.

*This paragraph presents a logical progression of ideas. Each sentence is related to the idea in the sentence before it, but each sentence also introduces a new idea that leads to the next one.

Finally, honors level P.E. would give students the academic reward they deserve for having athletic talent. This class would not separate the worlds of academics and athletics but bring them together. Students who might not be great at math or science could still improve their GPAs by doing a good job in P.E. These good grades would also show on their report cards for others to see. In the future, coaches and recruiters could see that the student took the extra step to take honors P.E.

It is clear that honors P.E. is a great idea. I hope it will go into effect and students will take the class more seriously than they do now. Honors P.E. would be more competitive, and the students who took it would be rewarded academically.

Chapter 7

TWO PRACTICE TESTS

Practice Test 1

Answer Sheet

PART 2: MULTIPLE-CHOICE QUESTIONS

THE BOY NEXT DOOR

1. Ⓐ Ⓑ Ⓒ Ⓓ   3. Ⓐ Ⓑ Ⓒ Ⓓ   5. Ⓐ Ⓑ Ⓒ Ⓓ   7. Ⓐ Ⓑ Ⓒ Ⓓ   9. Ⓐ Ⓑ Ⓒ Ⓓ
2. Ⓐ Ⓑ Ⓒ Ⓓ   4. Ⓐ Ⓑ Ⓒ Ⓓ   6. Ⓐ Ⓑ Ⓒ Ⓓ   8. Ⓐ Ⓑ Ⓒ Ⓓ   10. Ⓐ Ⓑ Ⓒ Ⓓ

STEPPING UP

1. Ⓐ Ⓑ Ⓒ Ⓓ   3. Ⓐ Ⓑ Ⓒ Ⓓ   5. Ⓐ Ⓑ Ⓒ Ⓓ   7. Ⓐ Ⓑ Ⓒ Ⓓ   9. Ⓐ Ⓑ Ⓒ Ⓓ
2. Ⓐ Ⓑ Ⓒ Ⓓ   4. Ⓐ Ⓑ Ⓒ Ⓓ   6. Ⓐ Ⓑ Ⓒ Ⓓ   8. Ⓐ Ⓑ Ⓒ Ⓓ   10. Ⓐ Ⓑ Ⓒ Ⓓ

PART 4: MULTIPLE-CHOICE QUESTIONS

GOOD CENTS

1. Ⓐ Ⓑ Ⓒ Ⓓ   3. Ⓐ Ⓑ Ⓒ Ⓓ   5. Ⓐ Ⓑ Ⓒ Ⓓ   7. Ⓐ Ⓑ Ⓒ Ⓓ
2. Ⓐ Ⓑ Ⓒ Ⓓ   4. Ⓐ Ⓑ Ⓒ Ⓓ   6. Ⓐ Ⓑ Ⓒ Ⓓ   8. Ⓐ Ⓑ Ⓒ Ⓓ

VIDEO VISIONARIES

1. Ⓐ Ⓑ Ⓒ Ⓓ   3. Ⓐ Ⓑ Ⓒ Ⓓ   5. Ⓐ Ⓑ Ⓒ Ⓓ   7. Ⓐ Ⓑ Ⓒ Ⓓ
2. Ⓐ Ⓑ Ⓒ Ⓓ   4. Ⓐ Ⓑ Ⓒ Ⓓ   6. Ⓐ Ⓑ Ⓒ Ⓓ   8. Ⓐ Ⓑ Ⓒ Ⓓ

PART 1

Explanatory Essay

Directions for the Explanatory Essay

This part of the practice test begins with an explanatory essay. After studying the prompt, you are asked to do a writing assignment. This activity tests how well you can organize your thoughts and express them in writing.

You have 30 minutes to complete this part of the test. Before you begin to write your composition, jot down your ideas on the prewriting/planning space first. Then write your response on the two pages that follow.

WRITING TASK

As part of a language arts class assignment, you have been asked to consider how the following quote is related to you.

"Men have become the tools of their tools."
—Henry David Thoreau

Write an essay explaining what this quotation means to you. Use details and examples in your essay. You have 30 minutes.

Prewriting/Planning Space

GO ON →

Written Response

After you have gathered your thoughts, write your response here and on the next page.

_____

_____

_____

_____

_____

_____

_____

_____

_____

_____

_____

_____

_____

_____

_____

_____

_____

_____

_____

GO ON →

GO ON →

PART 2

Narrative Passages

Directions for the Narrative Passages

In this part of the test, read the narrative passages. Then answer the multiple-choice and open-ended questions that follow. You can reread portions of the passage and make notes on the pages. You have 60 minutes to complete this part of the test.

The Boy Next Door

Ever since the fifth grade, Sean McCoy and I had to defend our friendship. Nobody believed that it was possible for a boy and a girl to be friends. I didn't either when I was nine. But the summer between fourth and fifth grade helped to change my mind. We had lived next door to the McCoys since right before my third birthday, but being neighborly wasn't really a top priority with my parents. They had eight kids to keep their eyes on.

Sean, on the other hand, was an only child, and when his mother turned ill that summer, his father didn't know what to do. I never asked what the illness was. All I knew, and all Sean would tell me, was that his mother stayed in bed most of the day and slept.

During that summer, I would watch Sean as he wandered around his big empty backyard, with his Yorkshire terrier, Winston, always at his side.

He would pump away on his solitary swing and climb the barren monkey bars.

Meanwhile, our yard next door was like the Wild West. We all wanted to use the swing set, which was frequently in disrepair. Dad typically had to fix it several times a week, because my younger brothers Timmy and Kyle had contests to see who could raise the set off the ground. We also averaged about five kiddie pools per summer, because my sister Mary liked to poke holes in them.

While Sean was busy fantasizing about having a big family like mine, I was wishing that I could have a big backyard like his all to myself. One day, I noticed him standing at the fence, watching all of us.

"You wanna come over and play, Sean?" I asked. "We're playing kickball soon."

Sean smiled. "Sure!" he shouted back, and he looked down at Winston. "Hey, Jenny, can I bring my dog?"

GO ON →

"Okay," I said.

Sometimes now, as I watch my own children play with neighbors, I smile to think about how simple friendship is in childhood. It's very cut and dry. You make friends. You get in fights. You call people names. And then you forgive, make up, and play kickball. That's how it was with Sean. Getting older is so tragic, because friendship becomes so much more ambiguous.

When we returned to fifth grade that fall, all the kids in class noticed that Sean and I were friends. They saw us eating lunch together, and they laughed and pointed as we walked home from school together. We put up with the teasing for as long as we could— about two weeks—before it was time for us to go our separate ways. I went back to the lunch table with the girls, and Sean left school immediately to walk home alone. One day, I saw him walking two blocks ahead of me, the back of his red head unmistakable.

"Sean!" I called out. "Wait up!"

He turned around, looked at me, and looked all around to make sure no one else was watching.

"Hurry up!" he shouted.

I ran as fast as I could, so fast that my backpack smacked against my back with each stride I took. I caught up to him, red faced and breathless.

"H ---- Hi," I panted.

"So here's the plan," Sean said, walking briskly and waving at me to keep up with him. "Meet me at this corner every day. We can walk home from here and nobody will see us if we hurry, okay?"

I smiled, finally catching my breath.

"Okay," I said.

From that point until the seventh grade, Sean and I were secret friends. By the time middle school rolled around, it was cool to be friends with boys, so Sean and I were in the clear. We spent most of seventh and eighth grade constantly telling people that we were just friends, but we both knew we wanted to be boyfriend and girlfriend.

On the day of eighth grade graduation, which was supposed to be the happiest day of my life, I received the crushing news: Sean was going away to prep school. His parents had enrolled

GO ON →

him in an all-boys school in New England, the same school his father had gone to thirty years earlier. When Sean told me, I couldn't stop crying. All of my plans for high school were ruined. We were supposed to go to proms together and compete on the co-ed swim team. I had even hoped that we might have the same lunch period so we could go to Renzo's Pizzeria like all the upperclassmen did. Now all of those plans were shattered.

20 Sean left for his school in the middle of August. He promised me that he would write as soon as he got there. We kept up our letter writing until the middle of October, when I started going out with Robbie Cassidy. At that point, Robbie became the center of my life for the next year. He was a junior, and he had a car. When Sean came home for vacation that winter, I introduced him to Robbie, but they didn't hit it off. Robbie was a jealous type, and he definitely did not believe that boys and girls could be friends. Whenever I would hang out with Sean, I had to lie to Robbie about it, and I felt bad. What I didn't realize then was that I didn't feel bad for Robbie.

Sean stayed in New England that summer, taking a job as a counselor in training at a local camp there. By the time he came home for a few weeks, I was away visiting my aunt in New Jersey, licking my wounds from my painful breakup with Robbie. The next time I saw him was Christmas Eve of our sophomore year. I was helping decorate our tree, which is a last-minute activity in our house, when the doorbell rang.

"Look who's here, Jenny!" My mother accompanied Sean into the living room, holding a foil-covered serving dish. "He brought over some of his mother's apple-cranberry crisp!"

I put down my handful of tinsel and walked across the room. "Hey, Sean!"

Upstairs I could hear my brothers and sisters. Kyle was shouting, "Hey everybody! Sean's here!"

All of my siblings stampeded down the stairs, screaming and shouting. They surrounded Sean, hugging his legs and jumping up and down.

"Are you here to play with us?" Mary asked. "Grandpa gave us Chutes and Ladders!"

"No," Sean said, much to the disappointment of my younger siblings, who whined in protest. "I came to see Jenny."

GO ON →

28 "Ooohhh," chimed Kyle and Timmy who made kissing noises and hugged each other mockingly. "Cutesy wootesy!!!" Then they giggled and ran back upstairs. Once they had gone, I kind of wished they had stayed. It was awfully quiet again.

29 "So, how are you?" I asked, getting back to my tree trimming. Sean took the hint and grabbed some tinsel himself.

"Good," he said. "I'm home until January. Figured I'd come say Merry Christmas."

"Thanks," I said. Was it possible that this was the boy I could talk to about anything? Now it seemed that there was nothing but silence and empty talk between us.

"It was nice of your mom to make that apple crisp."

"Yeah, she loves you. She always asks about you. I think she always wanted a daughter. You know that summer when she was in bed the whole time? Well, she had a miscarriage. The doctor said it was a girl. It was always so hard for her and my dad to have kids, you know? By the time I was born, she had been pregnant five times. She got so depressed that summer, though. It made her so happy that we were friends. It still makes her happy."

"Wow," I said. "I never knew that. Thanks for telling me."

"Hey, I never knew it either until last year." He finished with his last piece of tinsel, put his hands in his pockets, and pulled out a small box.

"Merry Christmas," he said, handing me the box. I opened it. Inside were Mrs. McCoy's opal earrings.

"She was going to give them away," Sean said. "But I told her how much you loved them on her, and she insisted." He smiled awkwardly. "Feels kinda funny giving you used earrings." He laughed.

38 "No," I said, laughing too. "It's the best gift I've ever gotten. I love them. I'm putting them on right now." It surprised me that I didn't even need a mirror to put them in.

"Listen," Sean said. "While I'm home, you wanna go to a movie or something? Catch up?"

"Sure," I said, walking him to the door. "That would be great."

"Cool." He kissed me on the cheek, pointing up to the mistletoe above us. "It's a date," he said, and walked down the front path.

"It's a date," I said to myself, smiling, liking the way that sounded. So I said it again out loud, "It's a date."

GO ON →

Directions

Circle the correct answer for each question.

1. The contrast between Sean's backyard and Jenny's backyard primarily shows
   A. Sean's wealth and Jenny's poverty.
   B. Sean's loneliness.
   C. Jenny's hospitality.
   D. Jenny's lack of a pet dog.

2. Which of the following statements from the beginning of the story illustrates irony?
   A. "While Sean was busy fantasizing about having a big family like mine, I was wishing that I could have a big backyard like his all to myself."
   B. "I never asked what the illness was."
   C. "They had eight kids to keep their eyes on."
   D. "And then you forgive, make up, and play kickball."

3. The fourth paragraph reveals that the narrator in the story is
   A. a child.
   B. a teenager.
   C. an adult female.
   D. an adult male.

4. The narrator's statement that "friendship becomes so much more ambiguous" in paragraph 9 indicates what feelings?
   A. Children can be very mean.
   B. Adult friendships are harder than childhood friendships.
   C. Childhood friendships are more painful to end than adult friendships.
   D. Defining friendship is impossible for adults.

5. Sean and Jenny become "secret friends" because
   A. it is more exciting and adventurous than being friends out in the open.
   B. they want to eat at the same lunch table.
   C. it is popular to have a secret friend and everyone has one.
   D. they don't want to suffer the social torture of kids who make fun of them.

GO ON →

6. The passage "I didn't feel bad for Robbie," (paragraph 20) can best be restated as
   A. I felt bad for betraying Sean.
   B. I felt bad for lying to Robbie.
   C. I felt bad about having to lie.
   D. I didn't want Sean to know about Robbie.

7. Why does Jenny wish that her siblings had stayed in the room (paragraph 28)?
   A. She prefers their company to Sean's.
   B. She wants them to help trim the tree.
   C. She feels awkward being alone with Sean.
   D. Sean is clearly happy to see them all.

8. When "Sean took the hint" in paragraph 29, the narrator is referring to
   A. Jenny's hint to trim the tree together.
   B. Jenny's hint to get underneath the mistletoe.
   C. Mrs. McCoy's apple crisp.
   D. Jenny's wish for him to leave.

9. The earrings that Sean gives Jenny are a symbol of
   A. Sean's cheapness.
   B. Jenny's modesty.
   C. Sean and Mrs. McCoy's admiration of Jenny.
   D. Mrs. McCoy's charity.

10. Jenny's observation that "I didn't even need a mirror to put them in" (paragraph 38) indicates that
   A. Jenny is usually clumsy.
   B. Sean helped her put them in.
   C. Jenny is unusually talented.
   D. Jenny is comfortable wearing the earrings.

GO ON →

Directions

Read the question carefully. You must answer *both* bulleted entries.
Be sure to develop all ideas fully and completely, devoting one paragraph
to each of the bulleted points. Use the prewriting/planning space
to jot down key points before writing your response on the lined pages that
follow.

11. In this story, Jenny and Sean's friendship is challenged by several
factors.

- What challenges do Jenny and Sean face as they try to maintain their
  friendship? Use evidence from the story to support your answer.
- Aside from those identified in the story, what other situations can
  affect people's friendships?

Use examples from your own education and experience to support
your answer.

Prewriting/Planning Space

GO ON →

Prewriting/Planning Space

GO ON →

Written Response

After you have gathered your thoughts, write your response here and on the next page.

11. _____

_____

_____

_____

_____

_____

_____

_____

_____

_____

_____

_____

_____

_____

_____

_____

_____

_____

_____

GO ON →

GO ON →

Stepping Up

Ted couldn't wait. He had woken up at 6:00 that morning, and he just could not go back to sleep. Today was the day that his Uncle Luke was taking him to meet Ryan Ahearn, the starting pitcher for the Highview Herons. Ever since he was three, his uncle had taken him to the Herons games every summer. Now, for his ninth birthday, he was going to throw the first pitch and sit in the dugout with Ryan. What should he call him, Ted wondered, Ryan or Mr. Ahearn? He would ask his Uncle Luke.

Uncle Luke used to play for the Herons before Ted was born. Ted once heard his father say that Uncle Luke might have made it big if it had not been for Aunt Lydia.

3 "Once he met Lydia, his game went downhill," Ted remembered his father saying, winking at Aunt Lydia.

4 "Well, I told him," Aunt Lydia laughed, bouncing her daughter Aggie in her lap. "It was baseball or me."

5 Now Uncle Luke and Aunt Lydia owned a sporting goods shop in town. Ted loved to go into that shop. He loved the smell of the leather baseball gloves and the rubber tires. Everything in that shop was a picture of promise.

6 Ted tiptoed downstairs to the kitchen and poured himself a bowl of Honeycombs. As he crunched and munched, he thought about how he might introduce himself to Ryan Ahearn. He wondered if Ryan Ahearn would have any time to pay attention to him. Probably not. He would be focused on the game, most likely. Ted promised himself that he wouldn't stare at Ryan Ahearn, even if he did

GO ON →

6 think that Ryan Ahearn was the greatest pitcher of all time. Ted didn't know which one he liked better, Ryan Ahearn's curveball or Ryan Ahearn's fastball. Nobody understood how much he really loved Ryan Ahearn. In second grade, his teacher had assigned the class to write a letter to a celebrity. When Ted read his letter to Ryan Ahearn to the class, Jimmy Keane laughed.

"Do you wanna marry Ryan Ahearn, Teddy? It sounds like he's your crush. Why don't you try watching a real pitcher like Randy Johnson? He's in the *major* leagues."

8 Ted hated Jimmy Keane. Even more, he hated what Jimmy Keane was implying about Ryan Ahearn. Still, Ted wondered about it himself sometimes. Why *hadn't* Ryan Ahearn made it to the majors? He was great, and he had been playing for the Herons for almost ten years. Maybe, Ted imagined, Ryan Ahearn wanted to stay there. Maybe he liked playing in the minor league. Maybe he had gotten lots of offers to go to the majors but he declined. Yes, Ted decided, that was the story. Ryan Ahearn loved Highview so much that he would never go to the majors.

When Uncle Luke arrived at 10:00, Ted had everything waiting in the front hallway: his glove, his picture of Ryan Ahearn to be autographed, a camera loaded with film, and three packets of Big League Chew. Uncle Luke smiled to see how excited Ted was in his Herons gear. He couldn't wait to see Ted throw out that first pitch. It had taken a lot of convincing for Uncle Luke to get the permission for Ted to do it. It was a lot more difficult than he had originally thought it would be. However, all of those phone calls would be worth it.

As they pulled up in front of Heron Stadium, Ted could feel his heart racing. He couldn't believe the day had finally come. He wished his father could be here to see it, and he knew that Uncle Luke wanted the same thing. Ted's dad had died when Ted was five. Uncle Luke had been like a father to Ted ever since. He was the coach of Ted's little league team, and he and Aunt Lydia took Ted down to their shore house every summer. If there was ever a problem, Ted could always talk to Uncle Luke.

11 They entered the stadium through the special door marked "Staff Only." The corridor was cool. Ted could hear his footsteps echoing as he walked

GO ON →

alongside his uncle. As they neared the door of the clubhouse, Ted started to wring his hands together. Uncle Luke greeted each player and introduced Ted. Ted had never shaken so many hands in his life. He knew every player's name and number, but he had never seen so many of their faces up close. He realized after a few minutes that the only player he hadn't met yet was Ryan Ahearn. He turned to his uncle.

"Uncle Luke? Where's Ryan Ahearn?"

"You know, Ted, I don't know. Wait here. I'll go find out."

Uncle Luke walked around a row of lockers, and Ted heard bits and pieces of a conversation.

"What do you mean?"

"Special situation . . . out this week . . . "

"But my nephew . . . ."

"Luke . . . you know he's been on the injured list for the past week."

"He said he'd be here. My nephew . . . cancer . . . only a matter of months."

Ted could feel tears brimming up. He couldn't believe his Uncle Luke had told. He had promised Ted that he wouldn't mention the cancer. Ted hated it when he saw all the kids at the hospital get lots of care packages. He would watch in disgust as the kids would open autographed baseballs and albums from celebrities. He hated it when they used their cancer to get stuff. He didn't want to meet Ryan Ahearn because he had cancer. He wanted to meet Ryan Ahearn because he loved baseball. Uncle Luke came back around the row of lockers, his face downcast.

"I'm sorry, Ted," Uncle Luke said. "He's not here today."

"I know," Ted said, his voice stony. "Why did you tell, Uncle Luke?"

Uncle Luke sighed. "I'm sorry, kid," he said. "It was the only way we could get you in to meet him. Otherwise, he wasn't interested. I had to play the cancer card. Maybe they'll let us come back next week. But for now, I asked the manager if he could call Ryan Ahearn and let us talk to him on the phone."

Ted's heart sank. It wouldn't be the same. However, he couldn't say that to Uncle Luke.

"OK," Ted said, and they headed for the manager's office. The manager had already called Ryan Ahearn's number and had him on hold. He hit the red blinking button and handed Ted the phone.

"Hello?" Ted said.

GO ON →

"Hey there little fella," a groggy voice muttered.

"Mr. Ahearn?" Ted was unsure. Maybe they had dialed a wrong number.

"Yah, tha's me kiddo. Enjoy a game, akay? Great game, baseball, lotsa fun." The man on the other end of the phone yawned loudly, then laughed. "Sorry bout that."

"No problem," Ted said. "I wish I could meet you in person, but I guess that can't happen today. But I'm a big fan, and I really love the way you pitch." Ted waited for a response. Five seconds went by.

"Yah, well, uh, kid, just do your best in school and try your hardest. And don't worry about the cancer, kid. You can beat it."

"I can?" Ted asked, hopefulness ringing through his voice. "But the doctor said. . . ."

"Who's your doctor? I'll call him up and give him a piece of my mind. Wha does he know?" The voice on the other end of the line was getting more and more angry. Ted knew the conversation had finished before it had even started.

"Well, bye Mr. Ahearn, and thanks for talking to me."

"No prob, kiddo." Click.

36 "Bye," Ted said to the dial tone. He turned to face his uncle and the manager, and both of them were looking away. Ted understood.

"Uncle Luke?"

His uncle cleared his throat and turned around, "Yes, Ted?"

Ted could see his uncle had been crying. "Can we go sit in the dugout now?"

"Sure thing," the manager said, his voice a little too enthusiastic. "You still wanna throw out that first pitch?"

"What do you think Uncle Luke?"

Uncle Luke smiled back at Ted. "I think," he said, clearing his throat again, "I think it would be great."

That was why Ted loved his uncle. Uncle Luke could have said that it would have made his father so proud. He could have told Ted to live life to the fullest or some other dopey-sounding thing like that. Instead, he told him the truth. It would be great for Ted to throw out that pitch. It would be great for him to make himself proud.

They opened the door to the dugout and squinted at the sunlight.

GO ON →

Directions

Circle the correct answer for each question.

1. The dialogue between Ted's father and his Aunt Lydia (paragraphs 3 and 4) can best be described as:
A. resentful.
B. unkind.
C. mocking.
D. playful.

2. From an informed perspective of the entire story, Ted's reflection that "everything in that shop was a picture of promise" (paragraph 5) reveals his
A. hopeful appreciation.
B. love of baseball.
C. excitement about meeting Ryan Ahearn.
D. depressing outlook on life.

3. Ted's thoughts about meeting Ryan Ahearn (paragraph 6) reveal that Ted is
A. fearful.
B. nervous.
C. humble.
D. a pushy fan.

4. Ted's theory about Ryan Ahearn (paragraph 8) can best be summed up by which of the following statements?
A. Ted has an active imagination.
B. Ryan Ahearn likes to play in the minor leagues.
C. Ted likes to give people the benefit of the doubt.
D. Ryan Ahearn is not good enough to play in the major leagues.

5. Ted's wringing his hands together (paragraph 11) clearly illustrates his
A. excitement.
B. anxiety.
C. stubbornness.
D. edginess.

6. The dialogue between Uncle Luke and the coach (paragraphs 15–19) reveals not only that Ted has cancer but also that
A. the coach is unkind to Uncle Luke.
B. Uncle Luke planned to play in the game.
C. Ryan Ahearn is on the injured list.
D. Ted is angry with his uncle.

GO ON →

7. Which of the following statements best illustrates the reason for Ted's tears (paragraph 20)?
A. His uncle revealed a secret.
B. He misses his father.
C. He has cancer.
D. He won't meet Ryan Ahearn today.

8. How can Uncle Luke's statement, "I had to play the cancer card" (paragraph 23), best be paraphrased?
A. I had to tell them you had cancer.
B. I had to ask for their pity.
C. I had to threaten them with cancer.
D. I had to tell them I had cancer.

9. Which of the following examples from the story best illustrates that Ryan Ahearn was sleepy?
A. muttered speech
B. a yawn
C. an angry voice
D. hanging up the phone abruptly

10. The statement, "Ted understood" (paragraph 36) refers to what fact?
A. Ryan Ahearn's recent injury.
B. His struggle with cancer.
C. The embarrassment of Uncle Luke and the coach.
D. His throwing out the first pitch.

GO ON →

Directions

Write the answers to these questions on a separate sheet of paper. Be sure to write neatly and develop all ideas fully and completely.

11. Ted is different from others his age.

- How does the absence of Ted's father make him different from others?

- How does Ted's love for minor league baseball make him different from others?

Use examples from the article to support your answers.

Prewriting/Planning Space

GO ON →

Written Response

After you have gathered your thoughts, write your response here and on the next page.

11.

_____

_____

_____

_____

_____

_____

_____

_____

_____

_____

_____

_____

_____

_____

_____

_____

_____

_____

GO ON →

GO ON →

PART 3

Persuasive Essay

Directions for the Persuasive Essay

The persuasive writing task tests your ability to organize your thoughts and express them clearly. It is given on day two of the ASK 8.

You have 45 minutes to complete this writing assignment. Before you begin to write your composition, jot down your ideas on the prewriting/planning space first. Then write your response on the two pages that follow.

WRITING SITUATION

The cafeteria and student lounge in your school currently have vending machines for students' use. The catering company that runs the lunch program in your school does not want the vending machines because it takes away from their business. The catering company has told your district that they will not renew the contract for next year unless the vending machines are removed from the school. If a new catering company is hired, it will cost the district 25% more than it does to have the current catering company. This means that the prices of lunch will go up.

WRITING TASK

Your school newspaper is accepting letters to the editor on this topic. Write your letter, arguing for or against the removal of the vending machines. Give clear reasons for your viewpoint, and make sure to develop each of your reasons fully and completely.

Prewriting/Planning Space

GO ON →

Prewriting/Planning Space

GO ON →

Written Response

After you have gathered your thoughts, write your response on this page and the one that follows.

_____

_____

_____

_____

_____

_____

_____

_____

_____

_____

_____

_____

_____

_____

_____

_____

_____

GO ON →

GO ON →

PART 4

Informational Reading Passage

Directions for the Informational Reading Passage

This part of the test contains an informational reading passage and is given on day two of the ASK 8. Read the passage, then answer the multiple-choice and open-ended questions that follow. You may reread the passage and make notes. You will have 60 minutes for this part of the test.

Good Cents

Even though I received an allowance as a child, I believe that it was actually to my disadvantage. Giving a weekly allowance may seem like a good idea. It might even be the social norm. However, I believe that this practice hinders a child from being truly self-sufficient. The wish of every parent should be to make his or her child as independent as possible so that the transition to adulthood goes as smoothly as possible. Nonetheless, it is becoming more and more evident that a generation of allowance recipients is turning out to be the least financially responsible group of adults in the history of this country.

I was raised in an upper-middle-class town and given lots of opportunities to succeed. I sang in the chorus, played the leading roles in multiple plays and musicals, pitched for an undefeated softball team, and competed in the academic decathlon. Never in the course of my middle school or high school career did my parents push me to get a job. I was given $20 a week, which covered the cost of my lunch at school and the public bus ride home when I couldn't get a ride. If I was going out to the movies, I would ask my father for money and he would always give it to me without reservation. In the second semester of my senior year of high school, I received a scholarship letter from my college informing me that half of my tuition costs would be covered. As a result, the money my parents had responsibly budgeted for my college tuition went toward the purchase of my first car.

3   When I graduated from college, I moved back home with my parents for a while. After I got my first job, I decided to move into an apartment with my sister. This would be the first time in my life that I ever paid for rent, electricity, gas, and so on. I had never kept a budget before because I never had expenses. Any job I had provided me with some spending money for entertainment. I had never used money I earned to pay for real-life expenses.

GO ON →

3 Because of this, I started to get overwhelmed by the financial responsibility of being an adult. I charged a lot of expenses on my credit card. Before long, I had racked up thousands of dollars in credit card debt. To help solve the problem, I moved back home with my parents until I had paid all of my debts.

4 My situation is not unique, but it is the result of a poor choice made by my parents. This is not to say that I am not fully to blame for all of my mistaken behavior. However, I want to point out the common mistake that a lot of parents make with the best of intentions.

5 What parent does not want to provide for his or her children if it is possible to do so? It is inherent in the nature of parenthood to give your child the best of everything. However, there is some value to the saying, "Give a man a fish, feed him for a day; teach a man to fish, feed him for

life." My parents were always generous with me. I was never wanting for anything at all in my life. They gave me everything I needed. As an adult, though, I wish that I had learned how to budget as a child. Obviously, my parents knew how to budget. They could give each of their four children the education they needed to succeed. I wish, though, that I had taken the time when I was younger to ask my parents about how they made their financial decisions.

6 Recently, a friend of mine was asked by her son if he could get a Game Boy. She arranged a method for him to save the money by doing extra chores (outside of the standard household chores that are expected of him). He took three months to save up the money. When she took him to get his Game Boy, he had enough money to buy the Game Boy, three games, and a case to hold the Game Boy. To this day, he takes excellent care of his toy. He gets very upset if his sister uses it without asking his permission. I believe that if I ever had to save up to buy any of my toys, I would have taken better care of them. Today, I can see this same attitude applying to myself. When I bought my first car with my own money, I

GO ON →

6   took excellent care of it. When I paid my own tuition in graduate school, I got straight A's. Because I was financially responsible, I was also much more likely to take care of my investments. If only I could have learned this lesson at a younger age!

7   So what should parents do instead of giving an allowance? I'm not suggesting that parents make their children pay for everything themselves. Certainly, children cannot be expected to pay for their soccer uniforms, their math tutors, or other standard fees that apply to others their age. However, if a child wants an MP3 player, make a deal. Instead of hiring a landscaper to plant the flowers in the front, hire your child to do it. Give your child the option to earn babysitting money on Friday night instead of hiring your usual

7   caretaker. If your child is willing to clean out the garage or iron drapes, let him or her do it for a competitive wage. Maybe then that MP3 player will be handled with much more care or that cell phone she's been dying to get will seem all the more sweet because she truly earned it.

8   I believe that this financially responsible mentality will serve children better. It will help them to be responsible, and it will help them to separate their needs from their wants. If a child really wants something, then he or she will proceed to achieve that goal. However, if the child receives instant gratification for his or her request, then he or she will not be able to distinguish between needs and wants. If a child lacks this ability to distinguish what is necessary, it can be detrimental in the future.

GO ON →

Directions
Circle the correct answer for each question.

1. The tone of the opening sentence can best be described as
   A. surprising.
   B. compassionate.
   C. ungrateful.
   D. optimistic.

2. Why did the narrator's parents never push their child to get a job?
   A. They didn't want anything to interfere with academic studies.
   B. They felt that their child was too young to work.
   C. They needed their child's help at home.
   D. There was no financial need for their child to work.

3. The narrator gets a car because she
   A. saved up the money to buy it herself.
   B. benefits from her parents' responsible budgeting.
   C. has to get to work every day.
   D. doesn't like riding the public bus anymore.

4. Which of the following examples from the article best illustrates that the narrator was "overwhelmed by the financial responsibility of being an adult" (paragraph 3)?
   A. spending money on entertainment
   B. charging expenses on a credit card
   C. paying monthly rent and utilities
   D. moving into an apartment

5. The "common mistake that a lot of parents make" (paragraph 4), according to the author, is
   A. not providing for their children.
   B. providing too much for their children.
   C. providing unnecessary things for their children.
   D. teaching their children how to budget.

GO ON →

6. Which of the following is the best paraphrasing of the narrator's statement, "I was never wanting for anything at all in my life" (paragraph 5)?

A. I always needed things.

B. I never wanted anything at all.

C. I was never in need of anything at all.

D. I was spoiled all my life.

7. The brief story told in the sixth paragraph is told with what purpose?

A. to encourage parents to buy electronic toys for their children

B. to show how good budgeting habits can be formed early

C. to illustrate that children are more responsible than adults

D. to warn readers about the dangers of poor budgeting

8. Which of the following pair of items represents a "need" and a "want" (paragraph 8)?

A. dance school tuition and lunch money

B. band uniform and instrument rental

C. field trip fee and picture phone

D. movie ticket entry and concession stand money

GO ON →

Directions

Read the question carefully. You must answer *both* bulleted entries. Be sure to develop all ideas fully and completely, devoting one paragraph to each of the bulleted points. Use the prewriting/planning space to jot down key points before writing your response on the lined pages that follow.

9. Responsibility can be defined in many ways.

- According to this author, what does it mean to be financially responsible?
- How does the author illustrate that she has become financially responsible?

Use examples from the article to support the ideas in each of your two paragraphs.

Prewriting/Planning Space

Prewriting/Planning Space

GO ON →

Written Response

After you have gathered your thoughts, write your response here and on the next page.

9. _____

_____

_____

_____

_____

_____

_____

_____

_____

_____

_____

_____

_____

_____

_____

_____

_____

_____

_____

_____

GO ON →

GO ON →

Video Visionaries

I arrive home after a long day at work, exhausted, hoping to unwind with a cup of tea and the 5:30 news broadcast. However, as I open the front door, I can already hear noises coming from the Play Station 2. I'll get my tea, but I'll have to wait until 6:00 for the news.

My husband, like a growing number of adult males, is a video game <u>aficionado</u>. He comes home after a long, hard day at work and turns on his Play Station 2. Today, he is playing the latest *Star Wars* game. He is Anakin Skywalker, and he battles with innumerable droids who try to close in on him. As he demolishes the last one, the round ends. He sets down his joystick, clearly satisfied with his success. He bounces up off the couch and heads into the kitchen to see what he can cook for dinner tonight.

Some people might find it silly, even immature, for a grown man nearing thirty to play video games. They might argue that such games should be reserved for the preteen and adolescent years. Nonetheless, I believe there is an argument to be made for the benefits of video games in the adult world. Video games, regardless of the age of the player, cultivate imagination, promote problem-solving skills, and provide a healthy mental avenue for coping with stress.

Albert Einstein is famous for saying, "Imagination is more important than knowledge." For a man whose career centered on logic, this might seem to be a radical statement. However, I believe Einstein was right. Although knowledge fills the mind, imagination feeds the spirit. Knowledge sometimes exhausts the mind, but imagination renews it. Thus, after a very long day at work, the last thing I want to do is *think* more. In contrast, *imagining* offers a great opportunity to me, as it does to my husband. He comes home with his mind filled with important <u>information</u>. Once he enters his imaginary video game world,

GO ON →

however, his mind is filled with his own <u>creations</u>. All of the "important" information is temporarily put aside. As Anakin Skywalker, he is in charge of his world, and there are no real consequences if he fails. Only in this <u>freedom</u> can a person truly be creative.

4

Aside from contributing to the creative impulse, there are other benefits to playing video games. Yet another perk to the video game culture is that it allows players to exercise good problem-solving skills under timed conditions. As Anakin, my husband must help R2D2 escape from the vicious grips of enemy droids. He must get out of the space station before he himself is captured. This translates to quick, on-your-feet decision making. Nevertheless, if my husband loses one round, he has the opportunity to try again and again until he gets it right. In the world of video games, you have limited time. However, you can

5

also have lots of chances to get things right if your time runs out. The do over opportunities offer reflection time to the player. During this reflection time, the player can ask himself, "What can I do better next time? What new approach can I take?" This <u>resilient</u> attitude can, in fact, strengthen the player's mind.

5

Finally, playing video games offers the adult player an opportunity to de-stress after a long day at work. In my husband's case, he may have had a few difficult customers today, the kind who yell and scream to get what they want. Perhaps as my husband plays Anakin Skywalker, he imagines that his problem customers are the <u>droids</u> he is destroying. With each fallen droid, he breathes a sigh of relief. By the end of his game, some of his daily troubles are forgotten, thanks to the imaginative benefits of his game. He is in a much better mood than he was when he got home. All it took was twenty minutes of playing a video game.

6

Even though video games can be expensive (this particular *Star Wars* one was $50), I support my husband's purchase of them. After all, I get $15 manicures, $30 pedicures, and $60 haircuts. Why shouldn't he get some pampering,

GO ON →

too? In fact, his pampering lasts much longer than mine does. It seems to me that he gets a lot more relaxation out of his time in front of the Play Station. Maybe the next time I feel like heading for the nail salon, I will pick up a joystick instead!

Directions

Circle the correct answer for each question.

1. The word <u>aficionado</u> (paragraph 2) most nearly means
   A. enemy.
   B. fan.
   C. rival.
   D. critic.

2. The mood brought about by the description in the second paragraph can best be described as
   A. downcast.
   B. violent.
   C. upbeat.
   D. uncertain.

3. Which of the following sentences best expresses the main idea of the article?
   A. Some people might find it silly, even immature, for a grown man nearing thirty to play video games.
   B. Some people might argue that video games should be reserved for the preteen and adolescent years.
   C. There is an argument to be made for the benefits of playing video games in the adult world.
   D. Video games, regardless of the age of the player, cultivate imagination, promote problem-solving skills, and provide a healthy mental avenue for coping with stress.

4. Which of the following statements would make a good argument against the main idea in the article?
   A. Adults who play video games are obviously immature.
   B. Video games should be played only by children.
   C. Adults should choose more age-appropriate activities for recreation.
   D. People of any age should be able to play video games.

GO ON →

5. What is the relationship between the <u>information</u> and the <u>creations</u> described by the author (paragraph 4)?

A. The information is a burden that the creations help to lift.

B. The information is necessary for the creations to exist.

C. The creations help to form the information.

D. The creations are a burden that the information helps to lift.

6. The <u>freedom</u> discussed by the author (paragraph 4) can best be described as a freedom to do what?

A. to follow directions

B. to learn new information

C. to escape reality for a while

D. to conquer a vicious enemy

7. Which of the following scenarios would stand in direct contrast to the world described by the author (paragraph 5)?

A. a baseball player who hits the ball out of bounds

B. a stockbroker who has ten seconds to make a trade before the market closes

C. a student who retakes a test after failing it

D. a runner who finishes a marathon

8. Which statement best summarizes the main idea of the final paragraph?

A. The narrator is more mature than her husband.

B. The narrator's husband likes video games.

C. The narrator supports her husband's choice of recreation.

D. The narrator believes that her husband's pastime is more beneficial to his well-being than her own pastimes are.

Directions
Write the answers on a separate sheet of paper. Be sure to write neatly and develop all ideas fully and completely.

9. In the article, the author's opinion about imagination is clear.

■ According to this author, why is imagination important?

■ How does using one's imagination benefit that person more so than using knowledge?

Use information from the text to support your answers.

GO ON ➔

Prewriting/Planning Space

GO ON →

Written Response

After you have gathered your thoughts, write your response here and on the next page.

9. _____

_____

_____

_____

_____

_____

_____

_____

_____

_____

_____

_____

_____

_____

_____

_____

_____

_____

GO ON →

GO ON →

Practice Test 1
Answer Key

PART 1: SAMPLE BODY PARAGRAPHS OF AN EXPLANATORY ESSAY RATING "5"

Man is separated from animals because he makes and uses tools. As man has evolved, his tools have evolved also. Tools now constantly require man's attention. Henry David Thoreau said, "Men have become the tools of their tools." He saw how much tools had taken over the lives of people around him.

First, think of Steve Jobs. He brought the computer into people's homes, and then he helped bring us the iPod, the iPad, and the iPhone. With these inventions, people now have phone, text, e-mail, and the Web in their pockets. However, once people have these, they are constantly checking them, especially the iPhone. It gives people freedom but at a cost. Steve Jobs gave us a tool, but we have become its tool.

Similarly, Henry Ford brought people the mass-produced automobile. The car gave us freedom and mobility. Now, though, people spend hours washing and waxing their cars. Even more, people spend days working every month to earn the money for their car payment. The car brings them to work, but they must work to pay for it. The car makes people the tool of their tools.

In conclusion, Henry David Thoreau was right. People have invented incredible tools. However, tools now control people. People are now controlled by their tools. People truly have become the tools of their tools.

PART 2: NARRATIVE TEXT MULTIPLE-CHOICE ANSWERS

"THE BOY NEXT DOOR"

1. B	3. C	5. D	7. C	9. C
2. A	4. B	6. A	8. A	10. D

PART 2: SAMPLE RESPONSE TO QUESTION 11

Jenny and Sean face two major challenges to their friendship. Firstly, peer pressure has a definite influence. As Jenny admits at the beginning of the story, "Nobody believed that it was possible for a boy and a girl to be friends." Clearly, Jenny's statement indicates that both she and Sean had to deal with others who teased them about being more than just friends. The second factor that challenges Jenny and Sean's friendship is distance. Even though they grew up next door to each other, they both have to adjust to the change in their friendship when Sean goes away to school. As it turns out, "absence makes the heart grow fonder." Jenny and Sean eventually discover that their relationship is not perfect, but that it can stand up to these two challenges.

One thing that can affect people's friendships is family situation. From my own experience, this is true. My best friend and I almost stopped being friends because of his parents' divorce. When his parents separated, he didn't tell anyone, not even his closest friends, because he was embarrassed. He also hoped that his parents would get back together, which did not happen. Unfortunately, nobody knew why he was so angry all the time. After two months of him acting like this, I finally asked him what his problem was. To my shock, he told me about his parents. Once I understood his situation, I could be a better friend.

Score for sample response: 3

Reasons for the score:

■ The writer chooses relevant examples and uses several effective transitions to lead from one idea to the next.

▪ Compared to the first paragraph, the second paragraph is rushed. The writer is not as careful with word choice in the second paragraph. (Ex: "I finally asked him what his problem was." This would be better stated as, "I finally confronted him about his behavior.")

▪ The second paragraph lacks closure.

"STEPPING UP"

1. D	3. C	5. A	7. A	9. B
2. A	4. C	6. C	8. B	10. C

PART 2: SAMPLE RESPONSE TO QUESTION 11

One way that Ted is different from other kids his age is the fact that he does not have a father. Ted has to rely on others to be father figures in his life. One of these people is his Uncle Luke. "If there was ever a problem, Ted could always talk to Uncle Luke." Another person he considers a role model is Ryan Ahearn. "Nobody understood how much he really loved Ryan Ahearn." After Ted gets disappointed by Ryan Ahearn, however, he realizes who he really needs to rely on: himself. "It would be great for him to make himself proud." Unlike other kids his age, Ted is much more mature and self-reliant.

Another way that Ted differs from others his age is his love for minor league baseball. He is as excited to see the game as other kids might be to see a major league game, which shows that he is easy to please. He even tolerates abuse from his classmate who teases him by saying, "'Do you wanna marry Ryan Ahearn, Teddy?'" Finally, at the end of the story, Ted does not get angry at Ryan Ahearn for his weaknesses. He moves on and keeps his eyes on the sky. This shows that like the team he admires, Ted is also an underdog.

Score for sample response: 2
Reasons for the score:

- The first paragraph contains a lot of redundancies. Although the writer uses quotations, the writer continually restates the ideas of the quotations instead of developing the main idea.
- This writer relies on quotes too much. Quoting is a good technique that should be utilized, but overusing it shows lazy thinking.
- Three sentences in the second paragraph begin with the word *he*. An easy way to vary sentence structure here is to flip-flop a sentence. For example, "He moves on and keeps his eyes on the sky," can be flip-flopped: "While keeping his eyes on the sky, he moves on." This strategy cannot be used with every sentence, but try practicing it where it does apply.

PART 3: SAMPLE BODY PARAGRAPHS OF A PERSUASIVE ESSAY RATING "5"

In the news, we are constantly hearing about the rising rate of obesity and diabetes. It is true that students do eat a lot of junk food. However, parents should show their children how to eat healthy. They should guide their kids to make the right choices so that the machines can be what they were intended for originally—a supplement that offers the school some modest fringe benefits.

It is primarily the responsibility of parents to be good role models for their children. If a student is eating five bags of cheese puffs and drinking ten cans of soda a day, it is not the vending company's fault. If parents are concerned about their kids eating too much junk food, then they should pack a healthy lunch for their children and make sure that they themselves demonstrate a healthy lifestyle. The problem is not the vending machines—it is the parents who allow a vending machine to take the place of a healthy meal.

Vending machines should stay because there will always be special situations in which students will need them. The cafeteria isn't open during sports practices, and students will still get hungry and thirsty from all that exercise. Suppose that during school a student gets nauseous and needs to get a can of ginger ale. If there were no vending machines, then maybe that student would get sick when this could have been avoided. Sometimes, students have to make up a test during their lunch period. If they didn't bring a lunch, the vending machine is the only option they have. All of these situations are possible.

Finally, the vending machine companies give the school a lot aside from just chips and soda. The scoreboard in our gymnasium was given to us by the Pepsi vendor, and the new sound system in the auditorium came compliments of the Snyder pretzel company. Next fall, all the repairs to the track are going to be paid for by the vending companies. If it weren't for the business that our students give these vending machines, we wouldn't have any of these other great things.

For all of these logical reasons, vending machines should be permitted here in the school. They are—and have always been—a way to supplement students' nutrition, not replace it. Anyone who believes that vending machines pose a threat to a student's diet should stop blaming big business and point the finger at him or herself.

PART 4: INFORMATIONAL TEXT MULTIPLE-CHOICE ANSWERS

"GOOD CENTS"

1. A	3. B	5. B	7. B
2. D	4. C	6. C	8. C

PART 4: SAMPLE RESPONSE TO QUESTION 9

To be financially responsible means not to depend on your parents. The author asked her father for money too much. She says, "They gave me everything I needed." This quote is describing her parents. She had to move back home with them so she could pay all her bills. This was a good idea.

The other thing it means to be financially responsible is to rely on yourself. The author says, "If I ever had to save up to buy any of my toys, I would have taken better care of them." "When I bought my first car with my own money, I took excellent care of it. When I paid my own tuition in graduate school, I got straight A's." She relies on herself and she can take care of herself.

Score for sample response: 1

Reasons for the score:

- In these paragraphs, the writer just gives examples, but the writer does not explain why the examples are important.
- The first paragraph states that the focus is not depending on parents. Unfortunately, the writer spends time developing how the author depends on her parents. By the end of the first paragraph, the writer is negating the opening point.
- Although the second paragraph has some good examples, the writer includes too many quotations and not enough analysis. The quotes need to be edited down, and the writer needs to explain what the value is in relying on oneself.

"VIDEO VISIONARIES"

1. B	3. D	5. A	7. B
2. C	4. C	6. C	8. D

PART 4: SAMPLE RESPONSE TO QUESTION 9
"VIDEO VISIONARIES"

One reason that knowledge is more important than imagination is that knowledge makes people responsible. Before a person can imagine something, that person has to know something. Einstein had to know a lot of information. Later on he could like imagination. Although "imagination feeds the spirit," it does not provide a person with what he or she needs to survive in life. It is true that knowledge "exhausts the mind." However, without knowledge, what would the mind have?

An even better reason why knowledge is more important than imagination is that the real world requires knowledge more than it requires imagination. In video games, there are "lots of chances to get things right," but not in the real world! There are not a lot of second chances out there. In the real world, you can't blow up annoying people without getting punished. If you let yourself get ruled by your imagination and not by your knowledge, you could get into a lot of trouble.

Score for sample response: 4

What does the writer do well?

- Excellent incorporation of quotations.
- Only key parts of quotations are used, and those are related to the ideas that are being developed.
- The question requires the writer to challenge the author's original ideas. The writer takes the author's original ideas and proves them to be wrong according to the examples the writer provides. This is an excellent focus on the question.

Practice Test 2

Answer Sheet

PART 2: MULTIPLE-CHOICE QUESTIONS

LET'S MAKE A DEAL

1. Ⓐ Ⓑ Ⓒ Ⓓ   3. Ⓐ Ⓑ Ⓒ Ⓓ   5. Ⓐ Ⓑ Ⓒ Ⓓ   7. Ⓐ Ⓑ Ⓒ Ⓓ   9. Ⓐ Ⓑ Ⓒ Ⓓ
2. Ⓐ Ⓑ Ⓒ Ⓓ   4. Ⓐ Ⓑ Ⓒ Ⓓ   6. Ⓐ Ⓑ Ⓒ Ⓓ   8. Ⓐ Ⓑ Ⓒ Ⓓ   10. Ⓐ Ⓑ Ⓒ Ⓓ

THE GIFT

1. Ⓐ Ⓑ Ⓒ Ⓓ   3. Ⓐ Ⓑ Ⓒ Ⓓ   5. Ⓐ Ⓑ Ⓒ Ⓓ   7. Ⓐ Ⓑ Ⓒ Ⓓ   9. Ⓐ Ⓑ Ⓒ Ⓓ
2. Ⓐ Ⓑ Ⓒ Ⓓ   4. Ⓐ Ⓑ Ⓒ Ⓓ   6. Ⓐ Ⓑ Ⓒ Ⓓ   8. Ⓐ Ⓑ Ⓒ Ⓓ   10. Ⓐ Ⓑ Ⓒ Ⓓ

PART 4: MULTIPLE-CHOICE QUESTIONS

ACADEMIC DISHONESTY

1. Ⓐ Ⓑ Ⓒ Ⓓ   3. Ⓐ Ⓑ Ⓒ Ⓓ   5. Ⓐ Ⓑ Ⓒ Ⓓ   7. Ⓐ Ⓑ Ⓒ Ⓓ
2. Ⓐ Ⓑ Ⓒ Ⓓ   4. Ⓐ Ⓑ Ⓒ Ⓓ   6. Ⓐ Ⓑ Ⓒ Ⓓ   8. Ⓐ Ⓑ Ⓒ Ⓓ

BAGEL BONANZA

1. Ⓐ Ⓑ Ⓒ Ⓓ   3. Ⓐ Ⓑ Ⓒ Ⓓ   5. Ⓐ Ⓑ Ⓒ Ⓓ   7. Ⓐ Ⓑ Ⓒ Ⓓ
2. Ⓐ Ⓑ Ⓒ Ⓓ   4. Ⓐ Ⓑ Ⓒ Ⓓ   6. Ⓐ Ⓑ Ⓒ Ⓓ   8. Ⓐ Ⓑ Ⓒ Ⓓ

PART 1

Speculative Essay

Directions for the Speculative Essay

This part of the practice test begins with a speculative essay. After studying the prompt, you are asked to do a writing assignment. This activity tests how well you can organize your thoughts and express them in writing.

You have 30 minutes to complete this part of the test. Before you begin to write your composition, jot down your ideas on the prewriting/planning space first. Then write your response on the two pages that follow.

Directions: Jack is sitting in class one day when the intercom interrupts the teacher's lecture. To his surprise, his name is called, and he is asked to come to the office. Everyone in class turns and stares at him in astonishment. Jack gets up slowly and walks to the hallway.

Write a story about what happens next. You have 30 minutes.

Prewriting/Planning Space

GO ON →

Written Response

After you have gathered your thoughts, write your response here and on the next page.

_____

_____

_____

_____

_____

_____

_____

_____

_____

_____

_____

_____

_____

_____

_____

_____

_____

_____

GO ON →

GO ON →

PART 2

Narrative Passages

Directions for the Narrative Passages

In this part of the test, read the narrative passages. Then answer the multiple-choice and open-ended questions that follow. You can reread portions of the passage and make notes on the pages. You have 60 minutes to complete this part of the test.

Let's Make a Deal

After three long summers of mowing lawns and three treacherous winters of shoveling driveways, Joe had finally earned enough. He had $4,125.82 in his savings account, and the ad for the motorcycle said that the price was $3,800. He called immediately. A man named Gerard told him that the bike would be his if he got there with the cash as soon as possible. He told Joe that he couldn't make any promises, and lots of other people had called about the bike. If they came with the cash, he was going to sell, first come–first served. That phone call was last night. Never before had a school day gone as slowly as Joe's day did. It seemed as though all of his teachers spoke in slow motion. Even lunch, which usually flew by, dragged out. His friend Ed promised to drop him at the bank. Joe had to wait for him to get all of his soccer gear out of the locker room. The bank closed at 4:00, and Joe walked in the front door at 3:48.

Joe stood in the serpentine waiting line in the lobby of Cook Bank, his account card in his hand. He wished that he could take that much money from the ATM. However, the bank had a rule that you couldn't take more than $300 in one day.

3 There were only two tellers helping the customers, one of them at the drive-through window and the other inside the bank. Joe looked around the bank and saw five other employees sitting behind desks on the main floor. He wondered why some of them couldn't get behind the counter and help. Three of them were on computers, but it didn't look like they were doing anything like work. One of the women kept smiling and typing quick messages, probably to someone on her

GO ON →

buddy list. Another man used only his mouse: solitaire.

4 An elderly woman at the front of the line was monopolizing the teller, asking her questions about her balance and making the girl go make an enlarged copy of her checking balance so she could read it when she got back home. Behind the elderly woman was a mother with twin two-year-old boys who wailed incessantly about being trapped in their stroller. The boy on the right kept throwing his sippy cup to the ground. The one on the left was more out of the stroller than in, constantly heaving all his weight toward the wheelbase. Joe thought that the only person who was more frustrated than he was with the elderly lady was the mother, who guzzled the dregs of her extra large Dunkin Donuts coffee and threw the cup into the trash can full of crumpled receipts. •

5 Behind the mother of twins was a very official looking businessman on a cell phone. His hair was slicked back. He wore a charcoal gray suit with black tassel loafers. Along with everyone else in the bank, Joe would have appreciated it if the man wore a little less cologne. The man spoke a little too loudly to the person on the other end, so

5 loudly that Joe began to wonder if the man was as important as he looked. The lady standing behind the businessman in line wore an apron, and she held a bag that looked like a pencil case. The bag had a lock at the end of it, with its key already positioned to open it.

6 The bank security guard was an older gentleman. Joe highly doubted that in the event of an emergency, the guard would be able to do anything aside from holding the door for everyone to get out. Shuffling over to the front door of the bank, the guard took a bulky key ring from his pocket, found the front door key, and locked it from the inside. Outside, several customers tried to enter, discovered the door locked with customers still inside, and turned away, stopping briefly to give the guard a sour look. Joe was glad that he was on the right side of the locked door.

7 The guard opened the door to let the elderly lady out, tipping his hat to her as he did so. The mother of twins was finishing her transaction as the drive-through teller pulled down her screen. Outside, Joe heard several car horns honking in unison and then the screeching of tires. The drive-through teller pulled her jacket

GO ON →

and purse out from under the counter, punched her time card, and lifted the partition to let herself out. After saying good-bye to the guard, she took her leave. Joe began to suspect the worst.

7

The remaining teller finished with the mother of twins and looked up to the remaining three customers.

"I'm sorry, folks," she said to none of the three in particular. "It's four o'clock, and our systems are closed for the day. Our staff will be happy to help you first thing in the morning."

Every curse word Joe had ever learned was on the tip of his tongue. He looked at the businessman, who was still on his cell phone and heading for the door, and then at the woman in the apron who was visibly peeved.

"Hey Tami," the woman in the apron said. "Can I at least put this in your safe overnight?"

Tami, Joe thought. *Now I know her name. I can ask her to please, please do me this one little favor.*

Tami was now reaching for her jacket and purse. All the other bank employees were heading for the door.

"Excuse me," he shouted, "Tami? Would it be possible for me to make a withdrawal?

I got here as soon as I could after school, and I was waiting in line with everybody else. See, I really want to buy this motorcycle tonight, and it might not be around in the morning."

"I'm truly sorry, sir," she started. "But our systems are down for the day. Just out of curiosity, how much were you going to withdraw?"

"$3,800."

Tami laughed. "Oh, sir," she said. "If you wanted an amount that large, you would have had to call in advance for us to get it out of the safe. Nobody keeps that much in his or her drawer."

The guard tipped his hat to Tami, and with that, she was gone. Joe stood in the middle of the bank foyer. The guard looked him over kindly, shaking his head from side to side. Joe trudged toward the door.

19 to 27

"Not to rub salt in the wounds," the guard asked, "But what kind of bike is it? A Harley?"

Joe stopped, leaning against the door frame. Honestly, he thought, did this guy think he could afford a Harley?

"No," Joe said, trying to smile. "It's a Honda."

"Really?" the guard asked, genuinely interested. "What year and model?"

GO ON →

Joe took the classified ad out of his jeans pocket. Even after a day, the print had already faded. "It's a 2002 CB 570 Nighthawk. Black."

"Hmf," the guard replied, furrowing his brow. "Mileage?"

"18,000."

"Well," the guard said, "Sounds like you've done your research, my man. Good luck with it."

"Thanks, buddy," Joe said, crumpling the ad and putting it back into his pocket. "Have a good night."

"You, too young man."

At home, Joe barely ate any of his dinner. He thought about calling that guy Gerard, just to see if he could possibly hold out on selling the motorcycle until the next day. He decided to give it a try. Pulling the ad out of his pocket, he reached for the phone and dialed the number.

"Hello," he said anxiously, "May I speak to Gerard, please?"

"This is Gerard. May I help you?"

"Um, I'm calling about the motorcycle ad. . . ."

"Sorry, sir, that bike has been sold."

Joe hung up and sat in silence. Stupid guy. Stupid bank with its stupid rules. He kicked the wall and punched his mattress. The next time he saw an ad like that, he'd go and get the money first, even before he called. He went downstairs and looked through the paper again. There were no new ads, but there was another bike for sale for $4,200. He decided to go to the bank tomorrow and take out all of his money. He'd ask his father to loan him the rest.

The next day, Joe arrived at the bank at 3:30, in plenty of time to be helped. He made sure to call in advance and tell the staff that he would be making a substantial withdrawal. Until he saw the money in his own hand, he didn't realize how much of it there was. He thought of all the years he had worked so hard to earn all this. Now here it was, forty-one $100 bills in the palm of his hand. All of a sudden, he felt quite worried. What if he walked out of the bank and got mugged? That was highly unlikely, considering nobody had ever been mugged in this town. Still, he thought, maybe he should hide it. . . .

"How's life, my man?" the security guard came up to Joe from behind, patting him on the back. Joe jumped and shoved his money in his front pocket.

"Jeez! Oops, sorry," he tried not to seem too flustered. "I'm good."

GO ON →

"Going to buy a bike?"

"I hope so," Joe said. "I wanted to have the money before I called, you know?"

"Yeah, I know what you mean," the guard said. "You know, I have a proposition for you myself. I'm selling a bike of my own. It's parked right outside. Go check it out."

"Really?" Joe asked. "You're joking, right?"

"No, honest. Go take a look."

Outside in the parking lot, Joe saw it, neatly centered between the two white lines of a space, angled perfectly. As he approached it more closely, each of the details was unmistakable.

It was a black 2002 Honda CB 570 Nighthawk. He checked the odometer: 18,103 miles. No way, he thought. He turned around and looked back at the bank entrance. The guard was smiling, and then he began to laugh.

It occurred to Joe that he had never looked at the guard's badge very closely, but he could already guess his name. As he walked back to the bank entrance, each letter on the guard's badge came closer into focus. Joe stopped in front of the guard and smiled at him.

"All right, Gerard," Joe said. "Let's make a deal."

GO ON →

Directions
Circle the correct answer for each question.

1. In the first paragraph, Joe's slow day at school is the result of his
   A. fatigue after a long night.
   B. anticipation for school to end.
   C. dread about an upcoming test.
   D. academic laziness.

2. Joe's attention to the bank tellers (paragraph 3) reveals his:
   A. frustration with the lack of service to bank customers.
   B. curiosity about computers.
   C. desire to work in finance himself.
   D. ability to notice small details.

3. The description of the employees (paragraph 3) characterizes them as
   A. rude to the tellers.
   B. untrained as tellers.
   C. attentive to the customers.
   D. eager to end their work day.

4. What is the purpose of the description of Joe's fellow bank customers (paragraphs 4–5)?
   A. It captures Joe's frustration.
   B. It reveals Joe's harsh criticism.
   C. It creates compassion for the mother of the twins.
   D. It characterizes the man on the cell phone.

5. Why does the guard lock customers out of the bank (paragraph 6)?
   A. The teller orders him to do so.
   B. He wants to get home as soon as possible.
   C. It is standard procedure for closing.
   D. He wants to speak with Joe in private about the motorcycle.

6. "Joe began to suspect the worst" (paragraph 7). This can best be restated as
   A. Joe doubted that he would be able to get his money.
   B. Joe believed his money had been stolen.
   C. Joe feared that the teller had misplaced his money.
   D. Joe did not feel safe.

GO ON →

7. In addition to the bank closing, Joe cannot make his withdrawal because
   A. he doesn't have it in his account.
   B. he needs permission from a parent or guardian.
   C. the bank needs advanced notice for a large cash withdrawal.
   D. the teller wishes to teach Joe a lesson.

8. The guard's curiosity about the motorcycle (paragraphs 19–27) makes sense later in the story because
   A. the guard buys the motorcycle and gives it to Joe.
   B. the guard himself is the owner.
   C. the guard is a motorcycle collector.
   D. the guard would like to buy a motorcycle for his son.

9. Joe's second visit to the bank differs from his first because
   A. he has now saved enough money to buy his motorcycle.
   B. the tellers are much more accommodating.
   C. he arrives early and calls with advanced notice of his withdrawal.
   D. the line is much shorter.

10. Joe's irrational fear of getting mugged (paragraph 35) is a greater reflection of his
   A. strong desire to spend the money.
   B. extreme paranoia.
   C. lack of trust in the bank employees.
   D. feelings of adult responsibility.

GO ON →

Directions

Read the question carefully. You must answer *both* bulleted entries. Be sure to develop all ideas fully and completely, devoting one paragraph to each of the bulleted points. Use the prewriting/planning space to jot down key points before writing your response on the lined pages that follow.

11. Sometimes people conceal information from others for a variety of reasons. In the story, Gerard does not reveal certain information to Joe.

- Why doesn't the guard reveal what he knows to Joe?
- Is it possible that Gerard wanted to keep the motorcycle for himself? Why or why not?

Use examples from the story to support your answers.

Prewriting/Planning Space

Written Response

After you have gathered your thoughts, write your response here and on the next page.

11. _____

_____

_____

_____

_____

_____

_____

_____

_____

_____

_____

_____

_____

_____

_____

_____

_____

_____

_____

_____

GO ON →

GO ON →

The Gift

It was habit for Cathy, the assistant at Marla's Bridal Boutique, to tell every female customer who tried on any dress that it looked great. So Karen wasn't surprised when she came out of the dressing room in her strapless hot pink nightmare of a bridesmaid dress and Cathy teemed over with <u>false exuberance</u>.

"Oh, sweetie, that is cute as can be!" Cathy smiled and clapped her hands together. Karen thought she looked like one of those caricatures that were always getting drawn at bar mitzvah parties. "What do you think, Mom?" Cathy asked, turning to Karen's mother who was busy staring at her own reflection. She turned to look at Karen, pausing to choose her words carefully.

"Well," she said, pulling the train of her bridal gown behind her and walking over to Karen's mirror, "I think the hem needs to be shortened." With that, Karen's mother pulled up the skirt until Karen thought she was going to have the hem up at her knee.

"I agree," Cathy said, attaching her pin cushion to her wrist. "Let's get started pinning, young lady! There's only two weeks until your mom's big day, so we've gotta move on this."

Karen stood obediently still as Cathy folded up the material at the bottom. She didn't need any more reminders that she was shorter than her statuesque mother. She looked over at her mother, who was fluffing the train of her bridal gown with her foot. It was the type of gown that should have been worn by a twenty year old, one of those mermaid style dresses. Karen wondered why her mother insisted on having a fancy wedding. She was forty-five years old. If she wanted to get married again, why didn't she do what all the other older people did and go to City Hall? Why did she have to have this big wedding on the beach with a

5 hundred people and a clam-bake reception? Why did Karen have to be her bridesmaid? Why couldn't her mother just choose one of her friends?

6 "So," Cathy said to Karen's mother, "Is Karen your only bridesmaid?"

7 "Yes. And Cliff's son Daniel is going to be his best man!"

8 "Oh," Cathy oozed. "That is sooo adorable!"

Karen wondered why all the adults thought it was so adorable. It wasn't as if she and Daniel were going to be the ring bearer and the flower girl.

"And how many guests are you having?" Cathy asked. Karen wondered if Cathy really liked asking these questions or if they were standard with every customer.

"About a hundred and twenty," Karen's mother answered. "Nothing too much."

Yeah, right, Karen thought. Last night, she had watched as her mother and Cliff did their calculations. By the end of their wedding, they were going to be in debt by about $10,000. Nothing too much, though. Karen won-

dered how she was going to go to college in two years when all of her child support payments had probably gone to pay for her mother's wedding.

When they arrived home, Cliff had already made dinner. Karen hated how her mother made such a big deal out of the fact that Cliff cooked. He had lived on his own for over twenty years now, so how was it such a big surprise that he cooked? He had to eat, didn't he?

They sat down at the dinner table, and the usual discussion ensued. "So, Cliff, how was your day?" Karen's mother asked.

"Good. I met my sales quota. My boss is happy. He took me out to lunch. How about you?"

"Well," Karen's mother said, leaning in to Cliff as though she were about to disclose the secret of the century, "One of the shampoo girls told me that she heard that Craig is selling the shop."

Cliff's eyes widened, "Really?" he asked intensely. Karen really hoped that this was not the exciting life of being an adult.

"Really," her mother said. "She said he wants to move to Myrtle Beach and open a place down

GO ON →

there. So who knows, maybe I'll have a new boss soon."

"Isn't Craig always talking about moving off somewhere?" Karen asked, looking down at her plate. "I mean, wasn't it Miami last month and Denver last year?"

Her mother's smile faded, "Yes," she admitted. "He does like to dream about escaping."

Finally, Karen thought. *Silence at the dinner table.* She heard nothing but the crunching of taco shells and chewing noises. That was all she wanted—no more happy family discussion. She cleared the plates, packed the dishwasher, washed the pots, and headed to her room. Maybe her friend Jamie was online.

She checked her e-mail and found nothing new. All of her friends had away messages posted. All of her homework was done, at least what she wanted to get done. She heard a chiming coming from her computer. Maybe Jamie had signed on. Karen looked at the screen name: ddnn2475. Who the heck was that?

Karen, you there?

24 Should she message back? What if it was some creep? Maybe it was some guy from school who had a secret crush on her and had gotten her screen name. She'd take a chance.

25 to 32 *Yes, I'm here. Who is this?*

It's Daniel. You know, your soon-to-be stepbrother.

Karen growled. What was he doing messaging her?

I was wondering if you wanted to go in on a gift for my dad and your mom. I'm kinda low on funds.

Karen hadn't even thought about a gift. Why should she get her mother and Cliff a gift?

Sure, Daniel. What do you wanna get?

How's school?

No idea.

She stopped short. Was he actually asking her a personal question? In the three years since she had met Daniel, he never made the least effort to get to know her. Especially after he left for college to live in Pennsylvania, she saw him once a year on holidays.

Outside in the living room, Cliff had his arm around Karen's mother. They were watching *A Wedding Story.*

"Cliff," she said, putting her hands on her hips. "Did you ask Daniel to message me or e-mail? All of a sudden he wants to get to know me."

Cliff turned red and looked at Karen's mother. "You know, young lady," Karen's mother said. "I have had enough of this

GO ON →

smart-aleck behavior. Cliff is trying his best to welcome you into his family. If you don't appreciate that, it's your problem. But don't make him feel stupid for trying to be nice."

"If he wants to be nice, he can leave me alone," Karen said. "He shouldn't try so hard."

38 "He tries hard because you make it hard to like you. You walk in here with a sour puss every day. You don't talk to us, and when you do, it's to make some nasty, sarcastic remark about something. Why don't *you* try being friends with you sometimes? It's really hard!"

Karen ran back to her room, slamming the door behind her. She hated her mother. She especially hated that her mother was right. She had been acting like a brat ever since her mother had gotten engaged. It just wasn't fair. It wasn't fair that her mother had a boyfriend and she didn't. It wasn't fair that after years of not having a father around and managing fine without him, Karen's mother suddenly needed a man around the house. Karen sat down on her bed and began to cry. She didn't even know why she was crying, really. Maybe she was crying because she missed a father

she hadn't ever known. Now she was getting a father that she couldn't even choose.

She thought about that again. She was getting a father that she couldn't even choose. However, wasn't that true about her biological father? She didn't get to choose him. She wondered if she would ever have chosen him. Would she have chosen a man who would have left her when she was three years old? What difference would it make now?

Her computer chimed again. She looked at the screen. It was Daniel.

Karen, you still there?
Yup. What's up?
Well, I found this power washer on E-Bay for fifty bucks. I think they'd both like that for the house.
Sounds good. I'm in!
Sure thing.

47 Karen opened her door and walked downstairs. Her mother and Cliff were back on the couch, looking deflated. They both looked up as she came into the room.

"Hey," she said, sitting down on the recliner across from them. "You're not gonna believe what Daniel and I are getting you guys for a wedding gift!"

Directions
Circle the correct answer for each question.

1. The <u>false exuberance</u> (paragraph 1) displayed by Cathy refers to
   A. Karen's moodiness.
   B. Karen's mother's bridal gown.
   C. Cathy's insincere compliments.
   D. Cathy's dislike of the bridesmaid dress.

2. The purpose of the conversation between Cathy and Karen's mother (paragraphs 2–8) is to
   A. show a lack of sensitivity on Karen's mother's part.
   B. describe the design of the bridesmaid dress.
   C. establish the timeline of the wedding.
   D. state that Karen is short for her age.

3. The word <u>oozed</u> (paragraph 8) most nearly means
   A. seeped.
   B. trickled.
   C. crept.
   D. praised.

4. Karen's thoughts during her mother's conversation with Cathy (paragraph 5) can best be described as
   A. insincere.
   B. nervous.
   C. cynical.
   D. dishonest.

5. Karen is happy to have silence at the dinner table because
   A. she is tired of listening to Cliff talk about work every night at dinner.
   B. she doesn't like that her mother gossips.
   C. she dislikes how much her mother and Cliff try to be like a happy family.
   D. tacos are her favorite and nothing should spoil the dinner.

6. Karen's reaction to getting an instant message (paragraph 24) reveals her
   A. lack of good judgment.
   B. snobbishness.
   C. resistance.
   D. hopefulness.

GO ON →

7. The messaging between Karen and Daniel (paragraphs 25–32) characterizes Daniel as
A. an older-brother-type figure.
B. arrogant.
C. romantically interested in Karen.
D. belittling to Karen.

8. Karen's mother's statements (paragraph 38) reveal that Karen's mother is
A. a complainer.
B. aware of Karen's manipulative behavior.
C. not affected by Karen's actions.
D. unaware of how Karen feels.

9. What is the most important realization that Karen experiences in the story?
A. Her mother and Cliff are spending too much on their wedding.
B. Her mother knows all of her tricks.
C. Daniel genuinely likes her and wants to be her friend.
D. Cliff will be a good husband and father.

10. Why are Karen's mother and Cliff described as <u>deflated</u> (paragraph 47)?
A. They are tired from all of their wedding planning.
B. They are emotionally exhausted due to Karen's behavior.
C. The cost of the wedding is too much to handle.
D. They are upset about their wedding gift from Karen and Daniel.

GO ON →

Directions

Write the answers to these questions on a separate sheet of paper. Be sure to write neatly and develop all ideas fully and completely.

11. The title of the story is "The Gift." On a literal level, this refers to the gift that Karen and Daniel plan to give their parents. However, titles can also be interpreted figuratively.

   ■ In what way is the gift a lesson that Karen learns?

   ■ In what way is the gift a feeling that Karen experiences?

   Use examples from the story to support your answers.

Prewriting/Planning Space

Prewriting/Planning Space

GO ON →

Written Response

After you have gathered your thoughts, write your response here and on the next page.

11. _____

_____

_____

_____

_____

_____

_____

_____

_____

_____

_____

_____

_____

_____

_____

_____

_____

_____

_____

GO ON →

GO ON →

PART 3

Persuasive Essay

Directions for the Persuasive Essay

The persuasive writing task tests your ability to organize your thoughts and express them clearly. It is given on day two of the ASK 8.

You have 45 minutes to complete this writing assignment. Before you begin to write your composition, jot down your ideas on the prewriting/planning space first. Then write your response on the two pages that follow.

WRITING SITUATION

In January, you return to school after your ten-day holiday break. On the Friday before you left for vacation, five out of your seven teachers allowed their classes to have parties to celebrate the upcoming vacation. In your homeroom, your teacher reads a letter addressed to all of the students, signed by the principal. The letter states that effective immediately, teachers are not permitted to have parties in their classes. The principal describes the conditions of the building when everyone left the Friday before the break. The carpeting in some classrooms has permanent soda and grease stains from pizza and chips. Some students left food in the hallways instead of properly disposing of it. As a result, there were rodent problems over the vacation. The principal states in her letter that parties are not for educational purposes, and she cannot endorse noneducational activities during class time.

WRITING TASK

Your language arts teacher has assigned the class to write an essay either supporting or challenging the principal's latest rule. You must give clear reasons for your viewpoint and make sure to develop each of your reasons fully and completely.

Prewriting/Planning Space

GO ON →

Prewriting/Planning Space

GO ON →

Written Response

After you have gathered your thoughts, write your response on this page and the one that follows.

_____

_____

_____

_____

_____

_____

_____

_____

_____

_____

_____

_____

_____

_____

_____

_____

_____

_____

_____

GO ON →

PART 4

Informational Reading Passage

Directions for the Informational Reading Passage
This part of the test contains an informational reading passage and is given on day two of the ASK 8. Read the passage, then answer the multiple-choice and open-ended questions that follow. You may reread the passage and make notes. You will have 60 minutes for this part of the test.

Academic Dishonesty

In today's technology-driven society, it is no wonder that academic dishonesty, or cheating, is on the upswing. Methods for cheating have become much more high-tech. Years ago, students used to write answers on their palms. Nowadays, a student is much more likely to cheat with a Palm Pilot. From text messaging answers during a test to photographing tests with a phone camera, the academic garden is full of fruitful cheating strategies. More than ever, teachers are creating tests or assessments that are "cheat proof." Some people believe that this is an effective way of dealing with the problem. Others believe that avoiding testing situations is not a practical or realistic way of dealing with academic dishonesty.

Many teachers believe that assigning take-home essays instead of testing students is a better way to assess them. After all, a student's writing is arguably the best representation of his or her knowledge. Or is it? Teachers who assign the same old essay topics are shocked to discover that some of their students steal and slightly alter essays written by older siblings that are still saved on the family computer. An even easier method of cheating on essays is to visit online study guides. Students can copy and paste portions of essays into their own writing. Plagiarism is not as black-and-white as it once was, but it is still running rampant in schools.

Dealing with the challenge of plagiarism is not easy. However, there are two avenues of approach to combat cheating. First, some teachers choose to assign essays only in class. Students are limited on time, and they must handwrite their essays under teacher supervision. This guarantees that the student is the only author. The second option that teachers often pursue is to have their students register their papers through an online plagiarism prevention site. Teachers will not read a paper unless the student's report comes up clean on the site's filters. Although each of these options sounds like

GO ON →

a practical solution to the problem of plagiarism, each has its disadvantages.

4   In-class essays are beneficial in that they prepare students for writing under timed conditions. This is especially helpful on standardized tests and in college. Unfortunately, not every student writes well under pressure. Teachers are faced with a pile of handwritten papers that are substandard compared with what they might receive if their students had time to word process them. In addition, revising is an important writing skill, but timed writing does not allow the student to revise his or her work.

Although online plagiarism screeners are an effective tool, they have their limitations, too. Firstly, some plagiarism screening sites are so sensitive that they report any use of online material. This means that if a student quotes the Pledge of Allegiance in his or her paper, the site will hyperlink that portion to the web address at which it is located. Virtually any possible sentence or phrase that has been used on the Internet can be traced. A student with no bad intentions can receive an unsatisfactory plagiarism report.

6   Another method that teachers use to deflect cheaters is project-based learning. In this scenario, students must create their own original project inspired by their studies. They then present their projects to the class. This method, too, has its share of shortfalls. For one, if a student works in a group, it is still possible for a student not to work and for the project to be completed. Even if the student works individually, a project can still be done well and not truly prove that a student has done a significant amount of work. Some students are gifted in front of audiences, and others are not. For those who tend to be more skittish when presenting, the project option puts them at a disadvantage. They may know the material, but they may not be able to express themselves as successfully as others.

7   It is evident that the problem of cheating is not one easily solved. Every day, good teachers do the

GO ON →

7 best they can to eliminate the possibilities of cheating in their classrooms. However, teachers are also quick to admit that they alone cannot catch every incident of cheating. What about students, especially the ones who don't cheat? Why are they less vocal about their cheating peers?

8 Nobody likes a tattletale, and few snitches make friends. The social implications of <u>whistle-blowing</u> are obvious. When a student reports a cheating incident to a teacher, he or she is looked upon by peers as a

8 self-interested brownnoser. The threat of being socially outcast is much greater than the threat of getting caught cheating. This is perhaps why so many students cheat and so few report incidents of cheating.

Academic dishonesty will always be a problem in schools. Over the years, it has taken on many forms and will continue to grow as technology grows. No matter how much teachers may try to conquer the cheating beast, it will always rear its ugly head.

GO ON →

Directions

Circle the correct answer for each question.

1. According to the article, which of the following examples is most likely to be a "cheat proof" evaluation?
   A. a take-home test
   B. a word-processed essay
   C. an in-class, timed piece of writing
   D. a project

2. According to other examples in the article, why might some people "believe that avoiding testing situations is not a practical or realistic way of dealing with academic dishonesty" (paragraph 1)?
   A. They believe that tests are the only proper evaluations.
   B. They don't believe that essays are ever truly honest.
   C. Testing situations are realistic and practical.
   D. Timed tests prepare students for college and standardized tests.

3. Which of the following sentences makes the best argument that the take-home essay is a good evaluation?
   A. Students need time to revise their work and improve it before submitting it for a grade.
   B. Students who work on take-home essays can get help from older siblings who have already done similar assignments.
   C. Take-home essays allow students to utilize online resources on their own time schedule.
   D. Take-home essays help reduce the stress level of the students.

GO ON →

4. According to the article, which of the following would not be an effective method for minimizing cheating?

A. handwrite essays in class under timed conditions

B. assign group projects instead of tests

C. screen essays through a plagiarism prevention web site

D. ask students to do individual presentations

5. Why are handwritten papers considered by some to be "substandard" (paragraph 4)?

A. All students' penmanship is poor.

B. Word-processed papers have a better appearance.

C. Timed writing is not as polished as writing that is not timed.

D. The pile of papers overwhelms the teacher.

6. Which of the following is not an example of a "shortfall" (paragraph 6)?

A. A student can join a group, do little work, and still get a good grade.

B. A student who knows the material may not present it well in public.

C. A group that works collectively divides the work evenly, and everyone gets a good grade.

D. A student who does not know the material still does a good job presenting to the class.

GO ON →

7. According to the article, why can't teachers "catch every incident of cheating" (paragraph 7)?
  A. They are naïve to the strategies their students use to cheat.
  B. There are many ways to cheat and few ways to assess students' knowledge successfully.
  C. They can't believe every tattletale they hear.
  D. They don't want to put their students in the awkward position of reporting their peers.

8. Which of the following statements best summarizes the idea, "The threat of being socially outcast is much greater than the threat of getting caught cheating" (paragraph 8)?
  A. Being hated by your friends is more threatening than being hated by your teacher.
  B. Students should take a chance and report a cheater.
  C. Everyone should protect each other from getting caught when cheating.
  D. Being accepted and making friends matters more than getting a bad grade.

GO ON →

Directions

Read the question carefully. You must answer *both* bulleted entries. Be sure to develop all ideas fully and completely, devoting one paragraph to each of the bulleted points. Use the prewriting/planning space to jot down key points before writing your response on the lined pages that follow.

9. In the article, the author discusses the benefits and drawbacks of methods used to deal with cheating in schools.

■ According to the article, what are the benefits of using a plagiarism prevention web site?

■ Even if a plagiarism prevention web site is used, how might it still not be successful in eliminating cheating?

Use examples from the article to support your answer.

Prewriting/Planning Space

GO ON →

Prewriting/Planning Space

GO ON →

Written Response

After you have gathered your thoughts, write your response here and on the page that follows.

9. _____

_____

_____

_____

_____

_____

_____

_____

_____

_____

_____

_____

_____

_____

_____

_____

_____

_____

_____

_____

_____

_____

GO ON →

GO ON →

Bagel Bonanza

My Ford Mustang smelled like a giant bagel with cream cheese. If you looked really closely, you could see poppy seeds and sesame seeds on the floor of my car. I worked in a bagel store in Bergen County, New Jersey. After waking up at 5:30 A.M. for my 6:00 A.M. shift, I would rush to get to work, my hair still wet, clipped up to the back of my head. When I arrived, Eddie, the bagel maker, had already been there for three hours. Even though Eddie functioned on little sleep, he was always cheerful and hardworking. I tried to be inspired by his early-morning cheer, but it was tough.

The immediate lesson I learned about life from working in the bagel shop was never to question people's idiosyncrasies. If a man wanted a cold hard bagel with extra butter, that is what you gave him, even if you knew butter was loaded with cholesterol and that man was already too fat for his own good. If somebody wanted extra ice in his iced coffee, even if doing so meant the coffee would get diluted later, so be it. If a lady wanted to put her own milk and sweetener into her coffee while there was a line going out the door, you opened up another carton of milk and helped the next customer until she was ready to be rung up. Finally, if someone asked for a tiny, little bit of cream cheese, you did not give that person a big blob, not unless you had a death wish.

The next life lesson I learned was that no matter how well you might plan something, never think that you are entirely in control. Once, I was getting ready to close. It was five minutes to four and I had wrapped all of the meats in plastic, cleaned out the meat case, disinfected the slicer, and put everything into the walk-in refrigerator in the back. Just as I was getting ready to punch my time card, a lady walked in and ordered an Italian combo with everything on it. This meant

GO ON →

unwrapping all the cheeses and meats, dirtying the slicer, and taking all of the condiments back out of the walk-in. As much as I had planned to get out of work at 4:00 on the dot, it was not going to happen. I closed up the store that day at 4:30. The cliché "the customer is always right" kept ringing in my head.

The Golden Rule also applied to the insights I gained from working in the bagel store. For example, nothing was more frustrating to me than having to open up the store when the person who closed the day before did not do a good job. Closing the store is an art. It requires that you think about the opening the next day going smoothly. At 6:00 A.M., I should not have to worry about starting the coffee from scratch, wiping down the counters, or stocking the drink refrigerators. These were all things that should have been done by a good closer. When I closed, I made sure to set up the coffee pots for the next morning so the only thing to be done was to hit the "on" switch. I stocked the refrigerator so that the warmer drinks that needed more time to cool were in the back of the refrigerator. In addition, I would also make sure

that the milk was stocked by its expiration date so that the later expiration dates were toward the back of the refrigerator. This required taking older cartons out of the refrigerator and placing newer ones behind them. I would always close the way I would like to be opened for, but not everyone shared my passion for consideration.

The funniest thing that I learned from working in the bagel store was that handling food can disgust you after a while. Even though I loved bagels, they were the last thing I wanted to eat at work. I was surrounded by bagels. I could have had any type that I wanted. After slathering cream cheese on fifty bagels or so, though, I had no desire even to eat. I can remember looking down at the grill, where I was preparing five bacon, egg, and cheese sandwiches at a time, thinking, "This smells so good, but I don't want to eat it." When I arrived home,

GO ON →

my mother would make me immediately put my clothes into the washing machine. I smelled of pork fat, cheese, and high-gluten flour. Cold cuts became not food but the hunk of stuff I had to put into the slicer to make a sandwich and send a customer on his or her way. The bagel store became like a factory. I had once loved to cook. Now that food assembly had become my full time job, cooking was the last thing I wanted to do. When I came home, I would eat whatever was convenient and filling as long as it did not require much preparation. Before that summer, I thought that I might want to be a chef. After all, I loved to cook and bake. Once I saw how much work it took just to run a deli, though, my culinary dreams were over.

Ten years later, I am eating bagels again. I stop by a different bagel store now. When I stop in at this bagel store on my way to work, I am glad to be a customer and not an employee. I have a lot of respect for the people behind the counter who have to multitask and keep a line full of customers happy. However, I won't forget all the lessons about life that I learned from working in the bagel store. They still apply to my life today, and they can

apply to any job. These lessons have helped me to accept people as they are, be flexible, value consideration, and understand that every job has its downside, no matter how much you might love it.

Directions

Circle the correct answer for each question.

1. The opening sentence of the article has an example of what literary term?
   A. alliteration
   B. rhyme
   C. simile
   D. personification

2. The purpose of the first paragraph is to
   A. establish a sense of the setting
   B. show how the narrator struggles with her early schedule
   C. describe the bagel-making process
   D. praise Eddie for his bagel-making talents

GO ON →

3. The word <u>idiosyncrasies</u> (paragraph 2) most nearly means
   A. peculiar habits.
   B. foolish actions.
   C. unreasonable demands.
   D. bitter insults.

4. The narrator's use of the phrase <u>not unless you had a death wish</u> (paragraph 2) can best be described as
   A. an actual occurrence.
   B. a threat to a customer.
   C. a wish for a higher-paying job.
   D. a dramatized statement.

5. Based on the last sentence of the third paragraph, how does the narrator feel about the earlier situation she described?
   A. It is personally inconvenient for her to do the proper thing in this situation.
   B. She is visibly frustrated with the last customer of the day.
   C. She is not willing to clean up after she makes the sandwich.
   D. She is happy to stay late and close properly.

6. Considering the information in the fourth paragraph, why is attention to detail so important to the narrator?
   A. She has a compulsive personality.
   B. She wishes to have the same consideration extended to her.
   C. There are hygienic hazards at stake for those who don't pay attention to small details.
   D. Customers always notice the little things.

7. Which of the following statements from the fifth paragraph best illustrates irony?
   A. Even though I loved bagels, they were the last thing I wanted to eat at work.
   B. I smelled of pork fat, cheese, and high-gluten flour.
   C. The bagel store became like a factory.
   D. Before that summer, I thought that I might want to be a chef.

GO ON →

8. Which of the following examples best illustrates that the narrator has been desensitized to food?

A. slathering cream cheese on fifty bagels

B. making egg sandwiches at the grill

C. cold cuts becoming a "hunk of stuff"

D. sending a customer on his or her way

Directions

Write the answers on a separate sheet of paper. Be sure to write neatly and develop all ideas fully and completely.

9. In this article, the narrator describes both the benefits and the drawbacks of her summer job. Choose any job, and answer the following questions about it.

■ What tough life lesson does this job teach you?

■ What benefit does this job offer you as a person?

Use examples from personal experience to support your ideas.

GO ON →

Prewriting/Planning Space

Written Response

After you have gathered your thoughts, write your response here and on the page that follows.

9. _____

_____

_____

_____

_____

_____

_____

_____

_____

_____

_____

_____

_____

_____

_____

_____

_____

_____

_____

_____

GO ON →

Practice Test 2
Answer Key

PART 1: SAMPLE BODY PARAGRAPHS OF
A SPECULATIVE ESSAY RATING "6"

Ms. Foy's lecture about averaging numbers seemed to be going on forever. Jack tried to concentrate and take notes, but his mind kept wandering.

"Jack Singleton, please report to the office."

Jack looked up from his notebook. Thirty sets of eyes were on him. He could see the wonder in those eyes, and he knew his eyes staring back at them had that same wonder. Ms. Foy said nothing as Jack got up and went to the door.

In the hallway, Jack's mind raced. What could it be? Why was he being called down?

At the door to the office, he could see Dan, his older brother, already sitting on the bench next to the secretary's desk. As he opened the door, Dan looked at him in surprise. "What's going on?" Jack said.

Dan shook his head. "I don't know."

The principal stepped out of her office. "Come on back, guys."

Jack let his older brother lead the way. They sat across from the principal. "Well?" she said.

"Well what?" Jack replied.

"We know it was one of you," Dr. DeFulvio said. "If whichever one of you did this confesses, then we'll only have to expel one of you."

"Did what?" Dan said.

"Broke into the school computer system to change the grades."

Jack sat back, amazed. "Dr. DeFulvio, I don't know the first thing—"

Dan cut him off. "It was me," he said.

Jack's chin hit the floor. "Dan?"

The principal looked at them both and said, "I'll give you a minute."

As she left, Jack said, "Dan, why? You have straight A's!"

Dan smiled sheepishly. "How did you think I got them? I'm good with computers. This time, I figured I'd change your average too. Sorry about that."

"My average?" Jack said. "Why change my average?"

The sound seemed to come from somewhere else. "Take the sum and divide it by the number of instances to get the average," Dan seemed to say. But it wasn't Dan.

"Jack Singleton, are you with me?" Ms. Foy said.

Jack looked around at thirty staring eyes. He smiled, relieved. "Yes, sorry, Ms. Foy," he said. At least he wasn't going to be expelled.

PART 2: NARRATIVE TEXT MULTIPLE-CHOICE ANSWERS
"LET'S MAKE A DEAL"

1. B	3. D	5. C	7. C	9. C
2. A	4. A	6. A	8. B	10. D

PART 2: SAMPLE RESPONSE TO QUESTION 11

Gerard obviously wants Joe to learn a lesson from his experience, which Joe does. Joe learns that he has to plan ahead and do some research. He learns not to expect any favors from anyone. He also learns that he has to deal with disappointment and bounce back. Gerard knew that if he told Joe who he was at first, then Joe would not have learned any of these important lessons. This is why Gerard responds by simply "shaking his head from side to side" instead of telling Joe who he really was.

Another possibility is that maybe Gerard changed his mind for a little while. Joe's desire for the motorcycle was strong.

He tells Joe, "Sounds like you've done your research, my man." Maybe when Gerard heard how much Joe really wanted it, he had to ask himself if it was really worth selling something that meant so much. In the end, he might have decided to sell because he saw how much joy it brought Joe to get the motorcycle.

Score for sample response: 3

Reasons for the score:

- As compared with the other quotations used in this response, the quotation used in the first paragraph is weak.
- Every sentence in the first paragraph begins with a noun or pronoun.
- Although the closing sentence of the second paragraph is good, there is not enough leading up to the closure to make it effective.

"THE GIFT"

1. C	3. D	5. C	7. A	9. D
2. A	4. C	6. D	8. B	10. B

PART 2: SAMPLE RESPONSE TO QUESTION 11

"The Gift" is actually Karen's realization that families can take on many forms. The only family that she knew in her life was the family she has with her mother. "After years of not having a father around," they were capable of "managing fine without him." When Cliff came into the picture, Karen had to change her perspective, which was difficult to do. Fortunately, Cliff is very patient with Karen, just like a good father should be. By the end of the story, Karen realizes that she has a father and a brother who care about her and that letting them into her idea of a family only makes sense.

Another interpretation of "The Gift" is Karen's newfound sense of gratitude. Throughout the story, Karen is extremely ungrateful for a lot of the things she has received. She sees herself as a victim because her father abandoned her mother and her. "She missed a father she hadn't ever known." However, she becomes grateful when she realizes that the "father" that she misses, her biological father, is obviously less of a father than Cliff, whom her mother chose. Karen sees that she is lucky to have Cliff.

Score for sample response: 3
Reasons for the score:

- The writer must stay in present tense. The first paragraph shifts between past tense and present tense, and this gets confusing. Even when the text quoted is in the past tense, keep all commentary in present tense.
- The quotation in the second paragraph needs to be incorporated more effectively.
- Closure on the first paragraph sounds awkward. It needs to be edited for clarity.

PART 3: SAMPLE OF A PERSUASIVE ESSAY RATING "6"

Parties are fun, but no one wants to clean up after them. Before we went on Winter Break, we had a big party to celebrate. Of course, kids get wild, and food got dropped, drinks got spilled, and trash ended up everywhere. When we returned to school after our break, we were confronted with what was left: a trashed school. I even saw a mouse run across the hallway in front of me as I went to homeroom. This is not the kind of school I or anyone else wants to go to! The principal is absolutely right to ban parties in classrooms.

First, there is the issue of families. In public schools, people come from different backgrounds and religions. While most of the students here are Christian, many are not. Is it fair that teachers throw Christmas time parties? How do those students who don't celebrate Christmas feel? Our school is supposed to be a welcoming place for all people, but when we have parties that celebrate only one group, we are excluding others. The only way to stop this is to ban parties in school.

Next, schools these days have serious money problems. With budget cuts, the school has to run efficiently. Now, however, the school must spend a great deal of money cleaning carpets, removing trash, and exterminating rodents and bugs that were attracted to the school from the party. What will the school have to cut to keep the budget in balance? Will the principal have to cut a spring sport or the spring play? Will the eighth grade class trip be cut, and if so, will the party have been worth it? Of course not, and to prevent something like this in the future, the principal is right to ban parties.

The last issue that arises from the parties is that of safety. School is supposed to be a safe environment. We constantly run fire drills and lockdowns to make sure it stays safe. The cafeteria is always clean, and now even hand sanitizer dispensers are available. But when students trash the school with parties, they make it unsafe. Mice, rats, and bugs are not only disgusting, they also bring disease with them. A dirty school is not a safe school. What's more, if students see mice running through the school, some will start to think it's not a nice place and make it even dirtier and more unsafe. Only banning parties can stop this.

The principal did not act in anger when she decided to ban parties in school. Instead, she looked at the consequences of the parties and made a good decision. Those parties might offend or exclude students and their families. The cleanup costs a lot of money the school cannot afford, and the parties have made the school unsafe. None of those things helped the school in any way. The students of our school must get over their feelings and look at the consequences of their actions. When they do, they will stand behind the principal's decision to ban parties.

PART 4: PERSUASIVE TEXT MULTIPLE-CHOICE ANSWERS
"ACADEMIC DISHONESTY"

1. C	3. A	5. B	7. B
2. D	4. B	6. C	8. D

PART 4: SAMPLE RESPONSE TO QUESTION 9

A plagiarism prevention web site has definite benefits. Students would have to upload their papers and essays to have them checked for plagiarism. As a result, they will definitely be afraid of getting caught. It is easy to try to sneak a paper past one teacher, but it isn't quite so simple to get a paper through a database. It is true that "this guarantees that the student is the only author." Students can no longer copy and paste from other sites.

Even though plagiarism screening is good, it also has drawbacks. Firstly, it eliminates any use of words from the Internet. Considering how enormous the Internet is and how much information in contains, it is impossible for anything to come up as 100% plagiarism free on a site that checks only Internet sources. Also, students may pay other students to write their papers for them. The site doesn't have any idea who the original author is, just who the author is who registers the essay. "Essays written by older siblings that are still saved on the family computer" may not be registered through the site. Therefore, the same type of cheating could occur.

Score for sample response: 3

Reasons for the score:

- The first paragraph is not as well developed as the second.
- The first paragraph needs better closure.
- The third sentence of the second paragraph could be edited for clarity.

"BAGEL BONANZA"

1. C	3. A	5. A	7. A
2. A	4. D	6. B	8. C

PART 4: SAMPLE RESPONSE TO QUESTION 9

A lesson I learned from babysitting is that life isn't perfect. Changing dirty diapers is not pleasant, but it is a job that has to get done. If it doesn't get done, the baby stays wet and gets a rash. Also, babies cry a lot. Sometimes you can't stop them from crying. You can burp them, feed them, or change them, and it won't make a difference. They will still cry, and you have to deal with it. The baby doesn't follow a perfect schedule. That's the same way that life is—there's no perfect schedule.

Another great lesson that babysitting teaches you is how to be responsible. The parent leaves you in charge of the house and the children, which is a lot to handle. You are responsible to make sure that no one plays with scissors or matches. If someone chokes, you are responsible to know the Heimlich maneuver. Thinking ahead is always a part of babysitting and being responsible. Saving babysitting money for college is one last example of being responsible.

Score for sample response: 3

What does the writer do well?

- ■ The writer establishes two clear lessons that babysitting teaches.
- ■ The writer uses clear examples from life to support and develop each idea.

How might the answer get a better score?

- ■ Try to use a few more transitions to guide the reader.
- ■ Do not overuse the same word. In the case of this answer, the word *responsible* is used far too much in the second paragraph.

Appendix

OPEN-ENDED SCORING RUBRIC

FOR READING, LISTENING, AND VIEWING

Points	Criteria
4	A 4-point response clearly demonstrates understanding of the task, completes all requirements, and provides an insightful explanation/opinion that links to or extends aspects of the text.
3	A 3-point response demonstrates an understanding of the task, completes all requirements, and provides some explanation/opinion using situations or ideas from the text as support.
2	A 2-point response may address all of the requirements, but demonstrates a partial understanding of the task, and uses text incorrectly or with limited success resulting in an inconsistent or flawed explanation.
1	A 1-point response demonstrates minimal understanding of the task, does not complete the requirements, and provides only a vague reference to or no use of the text.
0	A 0-point response is irrelevant or off-topic.

NEW JERSEY REGISTERED HOLISTIC SCORING RUBRIC

In scoring, consider the grid of written language	Inadequate Command	Limited Command	Partial Command
Score	1	2	3
Content and Organization	• May lack opening and/or closing	• May lack opening and/or closing	• May lack opening and/or closing
	• Minimal response to topic; uncertain focus	• Attempts to focus • May drift or shift focus	• Usually has single focus
	• No planning evident; disorganized	• Attempts organization • Few, if any, transitions between ideas	• Some lapse or flaws in organization • May lack some transitions between ideas
	• Details, random, inappropriate, or barely apparent	• Details lack elaboration, i.e., highlight paper	• Repetitious details • Several unelaborated details
Usage	• No apparent control • Severe/numerous errors	• Numerous errors	• Errors/patterns of errors may be evident
Sentence Construction	• Assortment of incomplete and/or incorrect sentences	• Excessive monotony/ same structure • Numerous errors	• Little variety in syntax • Some errors
Mechanics	• Errors so severe they detract from meaning	• Numerous serious errors	• Patterns of errors evident

Non-Scorable Responses*

(FR)	Fragment	Student wrote too little to allow a reliable judgment of his/her writing.
(OT)	Off Topic/ Off Task	Student did not write on the assigned topic/task, or the student attempted to copy the prompt.
(NE)	Not English	Student wrote in a language other than English.
(NR)	No Response	Student refused to write on the topic, or the writing task folder was blank.

Adequate Command	Strong Command	Superior Command
4	5	6
• May lack opening and/or closing	• Generally has opening and closing	• Has opening and closing
• Single focus	• Single focus • Sense of unity and coherence • Key ideas developed	• Single, distinct focus • Unified and coherent • Well-developed
• Ideas loosely connected • Transitions evident	• Logical progression of ideas • Moderately fluent • Attempts compositional risks	• Logical progression of ideas • Fluent, cohesive • Compositional risks successful
• Uneven development of details	• Details appropriate and varied	• Details effective, vivid, explicit, and/or pertinent
• Some errors that do not interfere with meaning	• Few errors	• Very few, if any, errors
• Some errors that do not interfere with meaning	• Few errors	• Very few, if any, errors
• No consistent pattern of errors • Some errors that do not interfere with meaning	• Few errors	• Very few, if any, errors

Content/Organization	Usage	Sentence Construction	Mechanics

• Communicates intended message to intended audience
• Relates to topic
• Opening and closing
• Focused
• Logical progression of ideas
• Transitions
• Appropriate details and information
	• Tense formation
	• Subject-verb agreement
	• Pronouns usage/agreement
	• Word choice/meaning
	• Proper modifiers
		• Variety of formations
		• Correct construction
			• Skills intact in:
			  • Spelling
			  • Capitalization
			  • Punctuation

NJ ASK 8 SCORING GUIDE

Writing:
a. Persuasive Essay: Score out of 6 x 2. (The essay is scored twice, so the total is out of 12. See Scoring Rubric on pages 215–216) _____

b. Explanatory or Speculative Essay: Score out of 6 x 1: (The essay is scored once, so the total is out of 6) _____

Reading:
a. Multiple Choice: 1 point for each correct answer
(Number correct out of 36 questions): _____

b. Written Response 1:
Score out of 4 (See 4-point scoring rubric on page 216): _____

c. Written Response 2:
Score out of 4 (See 4-point scoring rubric on page 216): _____

d. Written Response 3:
Score out of 4 (See 4-point scoring rubric on page 216): _____

e. Written Response 4:
Score out of 4 (See 4-point scoring rubric on page 216): _____

Total Points (out of a possible score of 70): _____

Converted Score (See Scoring Chart on page 218 to translate the score): _____

The Converted Score translates to (Circle one):
  100–199: Partially Proficient
  200–249: Proficient
  250–300: Advanced Proficient

SCORING CHART

Raw Points	Score	Raw Points	Score
70	300	34	210
69	298	33	208
68	295	32	205
67	293	31	203
66	290	30	200
65	288	29	198
64	285	28	195
63	283	27	193
62	280	26	190
61	278	25	188
60	275	24	185
59	273	23	182
58	270	22	179
57	268	21	176
56	265	20	172
55	263	19	169
54	260	18	165
53	258	17	161
52	255	16	157
51	253	15	154
50	250	14	150
49	248	13	149
48	245	12	145
47	243	11	141
46	240	10	137
45	238	9	133
44	235	8	129
43	233	7	125
42	230	6	121
41	228	5	117
40	225	4	113
39	223	3	109
38	220	2	105
37	218	1	102
36	215	0	100
35	213		

Index